Bloom's BioCritiques

Bloom's BioCritiques

JOHN STEINBECK

Edited and with an introduction by
Harold Bloom
Sterling Professor of the Humanities
Yale University

CHELSEA HOUSE
P U B L I S H E R S
A Haights Cross Communications Company
Philadelphia

Printed and bound in the United States of America.

10 9 8 7 6 5 4 3 2 1

Library of Congress Cataloging-in-Publication Data.
John Steinbeck / edited and with an introduction by Harold Bloom.
    p. cm. -- (Bloom's biocritiques)
Includes bibliographical references and index.
  ISBN 0-7910-6172-8 (hardcover) -- ISBN 0-7910-7115-4 (pbk.) I. Bloom,
Harold. II. Series.
  PS3537.T3234Z7154 2003
  813'.52--dc21
                                              2002155989

Chelsea House Publishers
1974 Sproul Road, Suite 400
Broomall, PA 19008-0914

http://www.chelseahouse.com

Contributing editor: Michael Price

Cover design by Keith Trego

Cover: Hulton-Deutsch Collection/CORBIS

Layout by EJB Publishing Services

CONTENTS

User's Guide

These volumes are designed to introduce the reader to the life and work of the world's literary masters. Each volume begins with Harold Bloom's essay "The Work in the Writer" and a volume-specific introduction also written by Professor Bloom. Following these unique introductions is an engaging biography that discusses the major life events and important literary accomplishments of the author under consideration.

Furthermore, each volume includes an original critique that not only traces the themes, symbols, and ideas apparent in the author's works, but strives to put those works into a cultural and historical perspective. In addition to the original critique is a brief selection of significant critical essays previously published on the author and his or her works followed by a concise and informative chronology of the writer's life. Finally, each volume concludes with a bibliography of the writer's works, a list of additional readings, and an index of important themes and ideas.

HAROLD BLOOM

The Work in the Writer

Literary biography found its masterpiece in James Boswell's *Life of Samuel Johnson*. Boswell, when he treated Johnson's writings, implicitly commented upon Johnson as found in his work, even as in the great critic's life. Modern instances of literary biography, such as Richard Ellmann's lives of W. B. Yeats, James Joyce, and Oscar Wilde, essentially follow in Boswell's pattern.

That the writer somehow is in the work, we need not doubt, though with William Shakespeare, writer-of-writers, we almost always need to rely upon pure surmise. The exquisite rancidities of the Problem Plays or Dark Comedies seem to express an extraordinary estrangement of Shakespeare from himself. When we read or attend *Troilus and Cressida* and *Measure for Measure*, we may be startled by particular speeches of Ulysses in the first play, or of Vincentio in the second. These speeches, of Ulysses upon hierarchy or upon time, or of Duke Vincentio upon death, are too strong either for their contexts or for the characters of their speakers. The same phenomenon occurs with Parolles, the military impostor of *All's Well That Ends Well*. Utterly disgraced, he nevertheless affirms: "Simply the thing I am/Shall make me live."

In Shakespeare, more even than in his peers, Dante and Cervantes, meaning always starts itself again through excess or overflow. The strongest of Shakespeare's creatures—Falstaff, Hamlet, Iago, Lear, Cleopatra—have an exuberance that is fiercer than their plays can contain. If Ben Jonson was at all correct in his complaint that "Shakespeare wanted art," it could have been only in a sense that he may not have intended. Where do the personalities of Falstaff or Hamlet touch a limit? What was it in Shakespeare that made the two parts of *Henry IV* and *Hamlet* into "plays unlimited"? Neither Falstaff nor Hamlet will be stopped: their wit, their beautiful, laughing speech, their intensity of being—all these are virtually infinite.

In what ways do Falstaff and Hamlet manifest the writer in the work? Evidently, we can never know, or know enough to answer with any authority. But what would happen if we reversed the question, and asked: How did the work form the writer, Shakespeare?

Of Shakespeare's inwardness, his biography tells us nothing. And yet, to an astonishing extent, Shakespeare created our inwardness. At the least, we can speculate that Shakespeare so lived his life as to conceal the depths of his nature, particularly as he rather prematurely aged. We do not have Shakespeare on Shakespeare, as any good reader of the Sonnets comes to realize: they do not constitute a key that unlocks his heart. No sequence of sonnets could be less confessional or more powerfully detached from the poet's self.

The German poet and universal genius, Goethe, affords a superb contrast to Shakespeare. Of Goethe's life, we know more than everything; I wonder sometimes if we know as much about Napoleon or Freud or any other human being who ever has lived, as we know about Goethe. Everywhere, we can find Goethe in his work, so much so that Goethe seems to crowd the writing out, just as Byron and Oscar Wilde seem to usurp their own literary accomplishments. Goethe, cunning beyond measure, nevertheless invested a rival exuberance in his greatest works that could match his personal charisma. The sublime outrageousness of the Second Part of *Faust*, or of the greater lyric and meditative poems, form a Counter-Sublime to Goethe's own daemonic intensity.

Goethe was fascinated by the daemonic in himself; we can doubt that Shakespeare had any such interests. Evidently, Shakespeare abandoned his acting career just before he composed *Measure for Measure* and *Othello*. I surmise that the egregious interventions by Vincentio and Iago displace the actor's energies into a new kind of mischief-making, a fresh opening to a subtler playwriting-within-the-play.

But what had opened Shakespeare to this new awareness? The answer is the work in the writer, *Hamlet* in Shakespeare. One can go further: it was not so much the play, *Hamlet*, as the character Hamlet, who changed Shakespeare's art forever.

Hamlet's personality is so large and varied that it rivals Goethe's own. Ironically Goethe's Faust, his Hamlet, has no personality at all, and is as colorless as Shakespeare himself seems to have chosen to be. Yet nothing could be more colorful than the Second Part of *Faust*, which is peopled by an astonishing array of monsters, grotesque devils, and classical ghosts.

A contrast between Shakespeare and Goethe demonstrates that in each—but in very different ways—we can better find the work in the person, than we can discover that banal entity, the person in the work. Goethe to many of his contemporaries, seemed to be a mortal god. Shakespeare, so far as we know, seemed an affable, rather ordinary fellow, who aged early and became somewhat withdrawn. Yet Faust, though Mephistopheles battles for his soul, is hardly worth the trouble unless you take him as an idea and not as a person. Hamlet is nearly every-idea-in-one, but he is precisely a personality and a person.

Would Hamlet be so astonishingly persuasive if his father's ghost did not haunt him? Falstaff is more alive than Prince Hal, who says that the devil haunts him in the shape of an old fat man. Three years before composing the final *Hamlet*, Shakespeare invented Falstaff, who then never ceased to haunt his creator. Falstaff and Hamlet may be said to best represent the work in the writer, because their influence upon Shakespeare was prodigious. W.H. Auden accurately observed that Falstaff possesses infinite energy: never tired, never bored, and absolutely both witty and happy until Hal's rejection destroys him. Hamlet too has infinite energy, but in him it is more curse than blessing.

Falstaff and Hamlet can be said to occupy the roles in Shakespeare's invented world that Sancho Panza and Don Quixote possess in Cervantes's. Shakespeare's plays from 1610 on (starting with *Twelfth Night*) are thus analogous to the Second Part of Cervantes's epic novel. Sancho and the Don overtly jostle Cervantes for authorship in the Second Part, even as Cervantes battles against the impostor who has pirated a continuation of his work. As a dramatist, Shakespeare manifests the work in the writer more indirectly. Falstaff's prose genius is revived in the scapegoating of Malvolio by Maria and Sir Toby Belch, while Falstaff's darker insights are developed by Feste's melancholic wit. Hamlet's intellectual resourcefulness, already deadly, becomes poisonous in Iago and in Edmund. Yet we have not crossed into the deeper abysses of the work in the writer in later Shakespeare.

No fictive character, before or since, is Falstaff's equal in self-trust. Sir John, whose delight in himself is contagious, has total confidence both in his self-awareness and in the resources of his language. Hamlet, whose self is as strong, and whose language is as copious, nevertheless distrusts both the self and language. Later Shakespeare is, as it were, much under the influence both of Falstaff and of Hamlet, but they tug him in opposite directions. Shakespeare's own copiousness of language is well-nigh incredible: a vocabulary in excess of twenty-one thousand words, almost eighteen hundred of which he coined himself. And of his word-hoard, nearly half are used only once each, as though the perfect setting for each had been found, and need not be repeated. Love for language and faith in language are Falstaffian attributes. Hamlet will darken both that love and that faith in Shakespeare, and perhaps the Sonnets can best be read as Falstaff and Hamlet counterpointing against one another.

Can we surmise how aware Shakespeare was of Falstaff and Hamlet, once they had played themselves into existence? *Henry IV, Part I* appeared in six quarto editions during Shakespeare's lifetime; *Hamlet* possibly had four. Falstaff and Hamlet were played again and again at the Globe, but Shakespeare knew also that they were being read, and he must have had contact with some of those readers. What would it have been like to discuss Falstaff or Hamlet with one of their early readers (presumably also part of their audience at the Globe), if you were the creator of such demiurges? The question would seem nonsensical to most Shakespeare scholars, but then these days they tend to be either ideologues or moldy figs. How can we recover the uncanniness of Falstaff and of Hamlet, when they now have become so familiar?

A writer's influence upon himself is an unexplored problem in criticism, but such an influence is never free from anxieties. The biocritical problem (which this series attempts to explore) can be divided into two areas, difficult to disengage fully. Accomplished works affect the author's life, and also affect her subsequent writings. It is simpler for me to surmise the effect of *Mrs. Dalloway* and *To the Lighthouse* upon Woolf's late *Between the Acts*, than it is to relate Clarissa Dalloway's suicide and Lily Briscoe's capable endurance in art to the tragic death and complex life of Virginia Woolf.

There are writers whose lives were so vivid that they seem sometimes to obscure the literary achievement: Byron, Wilde, Malraux, Hemingway. But most major Western writers do not live that exuberantly, and the greatest of all, Shakespeare, sometimes appears to have adopted the personal mask of colorlessness. And yet there are heroes of literature who struggled titanically with their own eras— Tolstoy, Milton, Victor Hugo—who nevertheless matter more for their works than their lives.

There are great figures—Emily Dickinson, Wallace Stevens, Willa Cather—who seem to have had so little of the full intensity of life when compared to the vitality of their work, that we might almost speak of the work in the work, rather than even of the work in a person. Emily Brontë might well be the extreme instance of such a visionary, surpassing William Blake in that one regard.

I conclude this general introduction to a series of literary bio-critiques by stating a tentative formula or principle for gauging the many ways in which the work influences the person and her subsequent, later work. Our influence upon ourselves is always related to the Shakespearean invention of self-overhearing, which I have written about in several other contexts. Life, as well as poetry and prose, is overheard rather than simply heard. The writer listens to herself as though she were somebody else, and the will to change begins to operate. The forces that live in us include the prior work we have done, and the dreams and waking visions that evade our dismissals.

HAROLD BLOOM

Introduction

February 27, 2002, was the centenary of John Steinbeck's birth. It would be good to be able to say, in this age of George Bush II, that the liberal and humane Steinbeck achieved permanence as a fiction-writer. Alas, rereading the best of his novels and stories is a very mixed experience. *The Grapes of Wrath* is a period piece, and inevitably will follow the path of all popular fiction, and will be read only by social antiquarians.

An ambitious writer asks to be judged alongside the strongest of his contemporaries. Try to read William Faulkner's *As I Lay Dying* in conjunction with *The Grapes of Wrath*. Steinbeck is obliterated, as he is by Willa Cather and Theodore Dreiser, Ernest Hemingway and Scott Fitzgerald, Nathanael West and Flannery O'Connor. This saddens me, because I *want* Steinbeck to have been a great writer on the Left. We lack such a figure, though Hemingway attempted to fill the lack in *For Whom the Bell Tolls*, and failed. And yet even his failures remain more readable than Steinbeck's popular successes.

The late Anthony Burgess, a wise critic and undervalued novelist, remarked that Hemingway was Steinbeck's trouble. Take "Oklahoma" out of the first sentence of *The Grapes of Wrath* and substitute "the Basque lands," and you could drop the book's first two paragraphs into several contexts in *The Sun Also Rises*. What Steinbeck thought to be his own quasi-biblical style is Hemingway all the way. What Steinbeck thought were his own portraits of enduring but frustrated women were D.H. Lawrence's. Compare Elisa Allen in "The Chrysanthemums," one of Steinbeck's better short stories, to March in Lawrence's "The Fox."

1

Influence without anxiety produces stagnation; a touch of the anxiety of influence might have benefited Steinbeck.

There are other difficulties in trying to reread Steinbeck with any rigor. The Okies of *The Grapes of Wrath* never were: Steinbeck knew Oklahoma about as well as he knew Afghanistan. That might not matter, except that Steinbeck's poor whites are contemporary with Faulkner's, and the Joads as a literary creation lack the aesthetic dignity and persuasive substantiality of the Bundrens in *As I Lay Dying*. Floyd Watkins, a quarter-century ago, demonstrated this, as well as the shadow quality of the Joads compared to the rural poor of Eudora Welty and Robert Penn Warren.

You can argue, if you wish, that Steinbeck's Okies are a visionary creation, but then you are likely to find them dwarfed by their cinematic representations in John Ford's *The Grapes of Wrath*, as superior to Steinbeck's novel as Herman Melville's *Moby-Dick* is in comparison to John Huston's filmed travesty of it.

Aesthetic defense of *The Grapes of Wrath* is perhaps still barely possible, but to get through *In Dubious Battle* now is a dreadful struggle. Steinbeck remains a popular writer, but so is the hopelessly, implacably doctrinaire Ayn Rand, dear to many rightwing readers. There are depths beneath depths in popular fiction: what should one make of John Grisham? I cannot force my way through more than a few pages. It is a sorrow that Steinbeck, a "worthy" writer, as Burgess said, should have fallen into the cosmos of period pieces.

ELLYN SANNA

Biography of John Steinbeck

A REALLY FINE BOOK

Shortly before the publication of *The Grapes of Wrath*, John Steinbeck wrote in his diary, "If only I could do this book properly, it would be one of the really fine books and a truly American book." Writing such a book greatly challenged Steinbeck; after all, he had to skillfully weave multiple characters and events together into a single narrative, and along the way, during the novel's development, he often doubted his abilities as a writer.

In addition to Steinbeck's insecurity, these months were generally turbulent. He and his wife bickered; he traveled restlessly; and both the American government and journalists suspected him of being a dangerous revolutionary. However, despite these difficulties, Steinbeck wrote the 200,000-word book quickly and smoothly. One way he achieved this was by writing while listening to calming, classical music—specifically, Tchaikovsky's *Swan Lake*, and Stravinsky's *Symphony of Psalms*. Steinbeck thus claimed to use "a musical technique," for writing that implemented "forms and the mathematics of music rather than of prose." To Steinbeck, the book was like a symphony.

Obviously, though, to write such an enormous book in a short period of time—between May and December, 1938—Steinbeck exercised immense self-discipline. As he worked on the novel, he wrote in his diary:

All sorts of things might happen in the course of this book, but I must not be weak. This must be done. The failure of will even for one day has a devastating effect on the whole, far more important than just the loss of time and wordage. The whole physical basis of the novel is discipline of the writer, of his material, of the language.

Thus, during these months, Steinbeck's mind seldom strayed far from *Grapes*. His friends noticed that he seemed to be almost in a trance when they talked to him, his thoughts clearly elsewhere, and even when he worked in his garden, his neighbors and family suspected that he was mentally working out some problem with the novel's plot.

Steinbeck had provided himself with a nearly impossible challenge, and at times, he found it overwhelming and discouraging. At first, his story exhilarated him, and the words flowed easily, but as months went by, depression and self-doubt consumed him. "I'm not a writer," he confessed once in his diary. "I've been fooling myself and other people." Yet despite his anxiety, he continued to write. "This one must be good. Very good," he told himself, and he held to a strict writing schedule, even when the words seemed stuck in his head.

Steinbeck's personal ambition was immersed in *The Grapes of Wrath*, but he also believed strongly in the story's subject. He wanted Americans to understand what the collapse of rural America really meant to those who suffered the most during the Great Depression. To this end, the story begins with a long description of the conditions in the Oklahoma Dust Bowl. In the southwestern Great Plains, the land had once been covered with grasses that held the soil in place through both drought and flood, but when farmers plowed the grass to grow wheat and raise cattle, they left the earth exposed. When drought hit the region, the soil began to simply blow away; at times, the wind picked up so much soil that the sky turned dark, and the wind-born dust was reported to have traveled as far as the Atlantic Ocean. In the Midwest, drifts of sand and dirt piled up against the houses, barns, and fences, while in other places, as much as four inches of soil were scoured away. This ruined acres and acres of land, forcing the farmers who lived there to give up their homes.

Such were the consequences of the Dust Bowl, the springboard of Steinbeck's narrative. But rather than focusing solely on the big picture,

Steinbeck chose to zoom in on the travails of one specific family: The Joads.

Steinbeck emotionally invested himself in these characters: Ma Joad, Tom, Rose of Sharon, and Casy. In his journal, Steinbeck claimed to "love and admire the people who are so much stronger and purer and braver than I am." Steinbeck knew that the characters needed to live and breathe if readers were to understand their lives, and Steinbeck feared his words would not describe them well enough. His wife, Carol, encouraged him to "stay with the detail," and it is indeed the characters' distinctive human qualities that demonstrate one of the novel's most noteworthy strengths.

In general, however, *The Grapes of Wrath* paints a bleak picture, for Steinbeck asks the reader to confront the reality of human injustice and helplessness. The novel tells the story of what Steinbeck calls "Manself" and describes the endless, and often hopeless, human quest for self-realization, both as a group and as individuals. But despite Steinbeck's plans and his disciplined, at times feverish, writing habits, the author had no title for his book for several months, until September 1938, when his wife drew his attention to this passage:

> The people come with nets to fish for potatoes in the river, and the guards hold them back; they come in rattling cars to get the dumped oranges, but the kerosene is sprayed. And they stand still and watch the potatoes float by, listening to the screaming pigs being killed in a ditch and covered with quicklime, watch the mountains of oranges slop down to a putrefying ooze; and in the eyes of the hungry there is a growing wrath. In the souls of the people the grapes of wrath are filling and growing heavy, growing heavy for the vintage.

Steinbeck thought this phrase, "the grapes of wrath," from "The Battle Hymn of the Republic" echoed his novel's tone perfectly; thus, he found his title, and his novel was complete.

On March 3, 1939 Steinbeck eagerly waiting for the mail, impatient to see his newest, longest, most ambitious book finally in print. When the package finally arrived, he tore it open and held the published edition of *The Grapes of Wrath*. 850 pages long, it was a thick, heavy book that was soon to spark controversy among critics. Some hated it, while others argued that it demonstrated the full maturity of Steinbeck's talent. Steinbeck himself wrote in his diary that he was "immensely pleased" with his book, which eventually brought him fame and fortune. Most of all, though, it proved to Steinbeck that he could, in fact, write a "really fine book."

AN ADVENTURESOME FAMILY

John Ernst Steinbeck III, born February 27, 1902 in Salinas, California, came from an adventurous and hardworking family; his people held fast to strong beliefs and acted accordingly. His Great-Grandfather Dickson, for instance, left Massachusetts in the 1840's to be an independent missionary to the Holy Land, hoping to convert Jews to Christianity. His plan, inspired more by religious zeal than any practical knowledge of either the Jewish people or the Holy Land, was to apply modern farming methods to the desert, causing it to bloom, which would, in turn, teach the Jews how to raise their standard of living. Out of gratitude for their newfound wealth, the Jews would be receptive to Jesus. However, in addition to the plan's overall lack of cultural sensitivity and understanding, the Dicksons' venture was plagued by terrible luck. They were shipwrecked on their way to the Holy Land, and once there, they found that their youngest son, who had gone over earlier, had died of tuberculosis. Furthermore, they learned that the Jewish people who lived there, in what was then a part of the Muslim Turkish Empire, were a persecuted minority who could not risk associating with Christians in any way. As a result, the Dicksons had no labor force to help them farm the land—unless they chose to use slaves. Great-Grandpa Dickson stuck to his principles, and he and his family nearly killed themselves carving a farm out of the desert by themselves.

Elsewhere, Steinbeck's paternal grandfather, Johann Adolph Grosssteinbeck—originally from Dusseldorf, Germany—traveled in the 1850's with his brother, his sister, and his sister's husband, a Lutheran missionary, to Jerusalem on horseback. There, the family met the Dicksons, and eventually, Johann Adolph and his brother married the two oldest Dickson daughters. (Almira was Steinbeck's grandmother.) The Grosssteinbecks stayed on to help the Dicksons with their farm project, and while Great-Grandpa Dickson must have been grateful for the help, his luck still had not changed. Bedouins attacked the encampment and stole everything the families had, and Johann Adolph's brother was killed. This was the last straw for the fierce old patriarch, and the two families abandoned the farm and traveled back to the United States. On the voyage home, sailors aboard the ship attacked the youngest Dickson daughter—she died from her injuries.

Eventually, Johann Adolph and his wife, Almira, settled in New England, where Johann Adolph became a woodcarver. By this time, he had dropped the "Gross" from his last name and became known as John Adolph Steinbeck. Then, just before the Civil War, the family moved to St. Augustine, Florida. When the war broke out, the Confederate army drafted John Adolph. He had no particular allegiance to the Southern cause, and at the first opportunity, he shed his uniform and escaped to the North. Once there, he and the Dickson family appealed to the Confederate government, and through the help of a kind Southern general, Almira Steinbeck and her children moved back to New England.

Ten years later, John Adolph traveled west to California, where he bought 10 acres of land near Hollister, 30 miles northeast of Salinas. By this time, he and Almira had five sons. After she and the children joined John Adolph in California, the family ventured into various potential careers—including dairy farming and raising fruit—before they settled on running a flourmill.

Steinbeck's father eventually became an accountant and a manager, working mostly for milling companies. He managed the Sperry Flour Mill in Salinas when his son, John, was born.

The maternal side of Steinbeck's family was as bold and daring as his father's, though less idealistic. His mother's father, Samuel Hamilton, was born in a North Ireland town called Ballykelly. Hamilton came to New York City at seventeen and married Elizabeth Fagen a year later. In 1850, a year after he was married, he took a ship around Cape Horn to California. Elizabeth followed a little later, traveling across the Isthmus of Panama, to arrive, and finally settle, in San Jose. The couple had nine children together: one died before they moved to California; one was born in New York and traveled to California with Elizabeth; six were born in San Jose; and one was born after they left. Steinbeck's mother, Olive, was among the six born in San Jose.

In the early 1870s, the Hamiltons moved out of San Jose, and after a couple years, began homesteading a ranch near King City, about 60 miles south of Salinas. Eventually, they bought a total of 1,600 acres of land, and even though the land was too dry to be much good for farming, Grandpa Hamilton made a decent living as a blacksmith, repairing and improving farm equipment. Olive, his daughter, became a schoolteacher, passing her county board exams when she was 17. A year later, she obtained a position in a one-room schoolhouse 15 miles south of Monterey, far north of King City. (She rode nearly 30 miles to work every day on horseback.) Eventually, she retained a position closer to home, where she met John Steinbeck's father, who worked for the Southern Pacific Milling Company in King City. The two fell in love and married.

Olive Hamilton Steinbeck, John Steinbeck's mother, was a strong woman, full of energy and determination. She was a friendly woman who loved to laugh, but she was also opinionated and always busy. Her son would later describe her unusual faith as "a curious mixture of Irish fairies and the Old Testament Jehovah." She had great ambitions for her only son, and she pushed him to achieve.

But unlike his mother, Steinbeck's father was quiet and somewhat withdrawn. His harsh blue eyes sometimes frightened people who did not know him, and he was a large but gentle man, with a sensitive nature. In the words of one of his daughters, Steinbeck's father "suffered for people in their trouble."

Steinbeck's father's ability to recognize the problems of others obviously influenced his son, as did the other strong figures in his family's line. But nonetheless, at an early age, John knew he wanted to follow a different path from the one his family chose.

A Boy with a Good Imagination

In Salinas, Steinbeck grew up in an ornate Victorian house filled with sisters. His two older sisters, Esther (ten years older) and Beth (seven years older), acted like apprentice-mothers toward John, while he came to feel closest to his baby sister Mary, who was three years his junior.

In 1906, when Steinbeck was four years old, his family witnessed the great earthquake of 1906, which destroyed much of San Francisco. Throughout Steinbeck's whole life, he would remember being taken down Main Street in Salinas by his father after the quake. He saw tons of scattered brick and broken glass, and a whole street full of rubble where the Ford & Sanborn Mercantile Store had once stood. Although Steinbeck's own childhood home escaped major damage, the chimney was affected most peculiarly by the quake: it had been twisted around completely. However, this irregularity was not at the center of Steinbeck's nostalgia; instead, he felt worse about his family's first phonograph; the quake knocked it on the floor so hard that it never played music again.

Most of Steinbeck's memories were not so traumatic, though. For his ninth birthday, his aunt gave him a copy of Malory's *Le Morte d'Arthur*. He loved the book and would lie awake at night, picturing the gallant knights in armor as they galloped from adventure to adventure. He and his sister Mary used wooden swords, cardboard helmets, and their pony while pretending to search for the Grail. They even invented their own secret language, using obscure words and phrases from medieval times.

Arthurian tales thus became a passion Steinbeck would never outgrow, sparking his study of Anglo-Saxon and Middle English, and eventually shaping his prose style as much, or more, than the King James Version of the Bible. And yet another consequence of Steinbeck's fascination with Camelot was the impressive collection of Arthurian books—one of the most extensive in the world, reportedly—that he amassed throughout his lifetime, extending far beyond his childhood.

As a child, though, Steinbeck's closest friends were Glenn Graves and Max Wagner, a boy who had grown up in Mexico—although his parents were American—and who told Steinbeck stories about what life was like across the border.

Together, the three boys organized a secret club that they called BASSFEAJ. It met in the Graves family's barn, and the letters stood for: Boys' Auxiliary Secret Service for Espionage Against the Japanese. The club required its members to wear disguises all the time and maintain total silence while on missions. Their stated duty was to find the home of every Japanese person living in Salinas Valley and mark the location with a cross on a map. Steinbeck even persuaded all the members to sign the constitution in blood. More than 50 years later, John Steinbeck recalled, with embarrassment, what happened when a Japanese-American boy, Takashi Kato, heard about the boys' secret society and begged them to let him join. Steinbeck ultimately had to confess to Takashi, one of his best friends, that the secret club was spying on

Japanese Americans and, therefore, couldn't accept him. The author remembered that Takashi was nearly in tears, blinking and mumbling, "Well, I want to join anyway. We can mark on the map where my father lives." Steinbeck grew so ashamed that he soon disbanded the BASSFEAJ. "It was a lasting lesson in racial friendship," he once recalled.

In spite of the club's dissolution, however, the boys continued to have adventures. Once Graves and Steinbeck caught lice from two tramps who had been allowed to sleep in the Graves' barn. Mrs. Steinbeck was horrified, making her husband scrub their son with a bar of yellow soap, harsh disinfectants, and a scrubbing brush. Steinbeck thought the cure was worse than any lice, though. He howled, through the steam, "But I want lice!"

On another occasion, Steinbeck found a bagful of tobacco stems that a neighbor claimed were so powerful, "they could blast oak stumps out of California hardpan." Steinbeck immediately called a secret meeting of his friends in his cellar. (He liked to call the cellar his "opium den.") One by one, the boys crept into the Steinbecks' cellar, where they rolled the tobacco in scraps of newspaper and lit up. They puffed away happily for a few minutes and then ran for the door, sick to their stomachs. When they went home, the boys' mothers were so alarmed by the sight of their green faces that the family doctors were called out in force. And although Steinbeck eventually resumed smoking, and smoked nearly all of his life, the other boys in the "opium den" that day avoided tobacco for years.

During the summer that Steinbeck was 10 years old, his father announced that he had a surprise. He took Steinbeck out to the stable, where he found a bay pony waiting in the box stall. The pony was named Jill, and Steinbeck's experiences with her laid the foundation for his short novel, *The Red Pony*.

But later, at age sixteen, Steinbeck became seriously ill with pleural pneumonia. During this time, his father worked through the day and then sat up with his son at night. Eventually, the doctor had to break through Steinbeck's ribcage to drain the fluid from his lungs. The nurses tried to gently prepare Steinbeck's father and mother for the worst, but Steinbeck's soft-spoken, sensitive father could not be shaken; he had had a premonition that his son would recover from the terrible illness. He told Steinbeck's sister, Esther, "John is going to live!" Steinbeck's illness reached the crisis point, but he survived, as his father had predicted. But for the rest of his life, even as an adult, Steinbeck was haunted by the memory of his illness. He always feared catching pneumonia again, and he worried a great deal about his own death. When discussing his battle with illness, Steinbeck demonstrates the fierce nature of his family's will:

> It came time for me to learn to walk again. I had been nine weeks in bed, and the muscles had gone lax and the laziness of recovery had set in. When I was helped up, every nerve cried, and the wound in my side ... pained horribly. I fell back in bed, crying, "I can't do it! I can't get up!"
>
> Olive fixed me with her terrible eye. "Get up!" she said. "Your father has worked all day and sat up all night. He has gone into debt for you. Now get up!"
>
> And I got up.

Two or three days later, Steinbeck's recovery was complete, and he grew furious when his mother wouldn't let him hike in the hills. "You're trying to make a baby out of me!" he complained, forgetting that she was the one who had mercilessly goaded him onto his feet in the first place.

Steinbeck's willfulness re-surfaced when he was a freshman in high school; he decided then to be a writer. He composed stories and short pieces and sent them to magazines, but he was so terrified of getting a rejection letter—or even an acceptance letter—that he never put a return address on his submissions. He just sent in his work and searched through magazine pages, checking to see if the editors had published what he wrote. They never did, of course, since Steinbeck hadn't even included his name.

Bearing this in mind, it's no surprise to learn that Steinbeck was extremely shy as an adolescent. As a self-defense mechanism, he pretended to be proud and aloof, but this, unfortunately, only made others dislike him. And things never really improved. As Steinbeck grew older, he came to hate the community where he had grown up. For him, the town of Salinas represented all the embarrassment and rejection he had experienced during his childhood and adolescence, in addition to being a narrow-minded, prejudiced, and hypocritical place. But Salinas never thought much of Steinbeck, either; even after he achieved fame, people in his hometown spoke of him with hostility.

After high school, Steinbeck happily escaped Salinas to enroll at Stanford University, intending to study English, and he attended the university, off and on, for six years—from the fall of 1919 to the spring of 1925. By ordinary standards, however, his career at Stanford was not a success. When he left the university for the last time, he had completed the equivalent of less than three years of full-time study. Incompletes, withdrawals, cinch notices (warnings of possible failure), and long leaves of absence badly tainted his academic record, and near the end of his college career, he sometimes didn't even bother to register for classes. Instead, he informally audited whatever courses appealed to him. Occasionally, he even forgot that he had already taken or audited a course until halfway through the semester.

Thus, Steinbeck's work inside the classroom was unremarkable, to say the least, and socially, Steinbeck did not do much better. When he first arrived at Stanford, he insulted a sophomore, nicknamed Shorty, by not carrying the student's bags when ordered to do so. It was customary for the sophomores to rule over the lowly freshmen, and Shorty's request was thus considered reasonable. But Steinbeck refused to be anyone's slave, and this snubbing of an upperclassman re-cast the die for Steinbeck's continued role as an outcast.

During his freshman year, Steinbeck also took a leave of absence to combat influenza. When he returned, in the spring of 1920, he passed Shorty on the way to his dorm room. Neither spoke, but Steinbeck felt he was being watched, and soon, after Steinbeck sat down at the desk in his room, the door flew open, and four sophomores came in. Steinbeck heard Shorty say three words: "Come with us." Steinbeck answered: "Not today." He had been expecting something like this, and he was prepared. From a drawer, he pulled a long-barreled .45 Smith & Wesson and placed it onto the desk in front of him. His visitors stopped in their tracks, and after a whispered conference and a few sidelong glances, they decided to retreat, muttering threats of retaliation as they went. (The gun lacked a firing pin, but the sophomores obviously didn't know that.) Of course, the incident did nothing to increase Steinbeck's campus popularity, but soon, more health problems would distract him from any social concerns.

In early May 1920, Steinbeck suffered an attack of acute appendicitis and left school for the rest of the term. That summer, however, he worked as a rodman with his roommate of the past year,

George Mors. George had told Steinbeck that it would be easy work, since all that rodmen were required to do was to hold up poles for surveyors. However, their first day of work proved more taxing than they expected. They lugged around heavy chains and cleared away heavy brush, filled with thorns and poison oak. Adding to their misery, the camp cook was the boss's wife and made wonderfully lavish lunches—but only for the boss. The lowly rodmen, meanwhile, had to eat food that was barely edible.

However, with the help of Steinbeck's father, Steinbeck and George soon moved to Salinas and got a better job in Spreckels—at the largest beet sugar factory in the world—which was a mere 20-minute, narrow gauge railroad ride away. Compared with their work at the survey camp, their new jobs were easy. They worked nine hours a day, six days a week, and earned $100 a month. But while working at the sugar factory, Steinbeck got metal filings in his eyes and had to be taken home with both eyes bandaged.

In the fall of 1920, Steinbeck returned to school, but he again fell into bad habits regarding his studies. He left the university once more, leaving a note stating that he had gone to sail to China. In spite of his exotic plans, however, Steinbeck proved unable to execute them; no one was hiring men who lacked experience, so instead, he worked, much less glamorously, as a clerk for a department store in Oakland, and then in a men's clothing store. Eventually, though, Steinbeck ended up working on a Spreckels ranch near Chualar, about 10 miles south of Salinas. He was a straw boss, supervising workers (though not the work gangs), and after the spring, he accepted a factory job in which he tested the ripeness of sugar beets.

Steinbeck became what's known as a "bench chemist" in the fall of 1922. Because sugar beets don't store well, they need to be harvested and processed in rapid succession; to this end, they were harvested from late August until mid-December, and during these months, bench chemists needed to work 12 hours a day, from 7 a.m. until 7 p.m. Steinbeck was in charge of 15-20 people and responsible for the equipment and the reactants. One of the reactants was alcohol, though, and early that fall, Steinbeck noticed that a great deal was missing. Since this occurred in the midst of Prohibition—when the sale and production of alcohol was illegal in the U.S.—Steinbeck suspected that someone was stealing the alcohol for personal enjoyment; to catch the culprit, he spiked the alcohol with phenolphthalein, a powerful laxative, and by the end of the shift, he had no doubt about who was to blame for the disappearing alcohol.

After this stint of work, Steinbeck re-applied to Stanford in November 1922. He provided letters of reference from his recent employers, hoping to prove that he had become more responsible, and the university allowed him to return in January 1923. This time, Steinbeck roomed with a young man named Dook Sheffield; the two men recognized each other as kindred spirits, and they remained friends for life. They had a similar sense of fun that added interest to Steinbeck's studies. For instance, in their shared room, they had an ugly wooden crate on top of a trunk. To disguise it, Steinbeck draped it with a cloth, creating a sort of dais, and, to give the platform added distinction, Dook stretched out more cloth over it in a graceful canopy, held up by wires. On the top step of this "altar," Dook and Steinbeck placed a foot-high Kewpie doll, dressed demurely in a white silk handkerchief. Steinbeck named her the Goddess of Chastity.

To cite a second example, the two discovered that when they turned out the lights, a can of Sterno placed on the lower step burned with an eerie, greenish flicker, so when they expected visitors, they lit the flame. Guests found the young men on their knees in the wavering shadows, facing the shrine with their hands upraised, their bodies swaying while they mumbled incantations to their goddess.

But as much as Steinbeck enjoyed these pranks, he still had no passion for his studies. Ultimately, he decided that he did not care whether or not he earned a university degree. Based on this decision, he attended only those courses that struck his fancy. He was going to be a writer, he reasoned, so why should he bother with subjects that wouldn't be any use to him? This philosophy displeased Stanford's administration, but eventually, they agreed to let Steinbeck attend only those courses he chose. Perhaps, by this time, they hoped that by humoring Steinbeck, he would finally just go away—which, of course, he did.

Thus, nothing in Steinbeck's childhood or adolescence indicated how much he would later achieve. Obviously, he had a good imagination, but his teachers and parents couldn't escape the notion that he lacked the discipline to apply it toward something lasting and worthwhile.

ROMANCE AND WRITING

Near the end of his time at Stanford, Steinbeck fell in love with a girl named Margaret Gemmell. Reputedly a conceited, snobbish girl, Steinbeck never came to know her well, for he was not yet looking for a relationship; he merely wanted someone to adore and put on a pedestal. However, Margaret became intrigued when she learned that Steinbeck aspired to be a writer, and she arranged to meet him at an English Club party; she was soon disappointed. She found Steinbeck too shy and thought he drank too much. Later, she recalled, "The entire evening, he talked to me about his leprechauns." But despite Steinbeck's awkward performance, the two discovered that they shared a class in common. They began walking to the class together, and Steinbeck eventually asked Margaret for a date. Their relationship continued for more than a year, and even after he left Stanford, he came back to see her. However, as Steinbeck's attachment to Stanford lessened, so did his feelings for Margaret. He felt like an outsider and a failure whenever he returned to the campus for a visit, and these feelings put a strain on the relationship, which ended outright when Steinbeck decided to leave California.

New York City was the only place for a serious writer, Steinbeck finally concluded. After all, that was where all the publishers and big-name writers lived and worked. He was not alone in feeling this way about New York, of course; at this time, Greenwich Village (in particular) seemed to shine with a magical, creative aura. Aspiring young writers, actors, and singers all took the pilgrimage, dreaming of fame and fortune. But this chance at success, as always, had a financial cost. Steinbeck, to earn money to move to New York, took a job working for a Mrs. Price, the mother of a friend's girlfriend. A recent widow, she owned and managed a holiday resort lodge on Fallen Leaf Lake, near Lake Tahoe in the High Sierras. She was happy to hire Steinbeck to mend windows and repair broken toilets; he also drove the lodge's Pierce-Arrow car each day into Tallac, a local village on Lake Tahoe. There, he picked up guests, shopped for odds and ends needed for maintenance duties, and picked up the mail. After Steinbeck saved his wages from this job, he finally boarded the freighter Katrina in November 1925, heading to New York City. He began the trip with $100, but by the time the ship docked in New York, he had only $3. He spent much of it on alcohol, while spending the rest attempting to impress a girl he met in Havana.

And when the freighter approached its final destination, the sight of New York from Steinbeck's porthole overwhelmed him: "There was something monstrous about it," he remembered later, "the tall buildings looming to the sky and the lights shining through the falling snow. I crept ashore—frightened and cold and with a touch of panic in my stomach." However, he was not all alone and penniless in the big city; his sister Elizabeth was already living there, and her husband lent Steinbeck $30 to get started.

Steinbeck soon obtained a job working on the construction of Madison Square Garden. For the next few weeks, he pushed 150-pound wheelbarrows of cement all day long. If he wanted to earn overtime—at the rate of $2 an hour—he worked 10 to 18 hours a day. Steinbeck, already a tall, husky young man, became more muscular from all the manual labor. But in contrast to the bright lights of Broadway, the partially built Madison Square Garden was as cold and dark as a cave. Construction lights strung along the scaffolds sent long beams down through the planks and gave the men just enough light to know where they were. Big "salamanders" of glowing red coals were set here and there on the ground so the men could warm their loads of wet mortar when they started to freeze. The cold and heavy work numbed Steinbeck's hands and feet, but he would stop occasionally to warm himself near the coals, grateful for the moment of rest.

One day, five or six weeks after he began the job, a worker stumbled on a scaffold, high up, near the ceiling. The man fell to his death, near where Steinbeck stood. Steinbeck looked down in horror and shock at the man's blood, then turned away and was violently sick. That night, he collected his check and never returned to the job, glad to be done with it. The work had been too exhausting, and he never had energy left for writing. According to his sister, "He couldn't even read the newspapers when he got home at night ... I'd give him a sandwich, and he'd go straight to bed, where he'd sit with a pencil and try to write a few lines. But he knew it would never work. You couldn't do that kind of physical work and think at the same time." Fortunately, Steinbeck's uncle, Joe Hamilton, who owned an advertising agency in Chicago, happened to be in New York on business at the time. He got Steinbeck a job as a reporter for the New York American, one of the papers owned by Hearst.

Of course, the work was far less physically demanding than the heavy labor he had been doing, but Steinbeck nonetheless hated doing general assignment work. He was too soft-hearted to persuade bereaved people to tell their stories without becoming emotionally involved himself, and he refused to stoop so low as to swipe personal photographs off people's piano tops. Even worse, his active imagination got him in trouble, because he couldn't help coloring the facts with his own fancy. Furthermore, when his superiors heavily edited or re-wrote his stories, he suffered emotional torture. It soon became clear that Steinbeck was not a journalist. A reporter needs to state the facts with the fewest possible words, and Steinbeck's writing style, packed full of metaphors and images, gave his editors headaches. After a month, they sent Steinbeck to report on the federal court, where he was taken under the wing of a crew of experienced court reporters.

These men helped Steinbeck learn to cut the fancy airs from his writing, training him to adopt a cleaner, simpler writing style. Even with this tutelage, however, Steinbeck's uncle's influence was the only reason he kept the job as long as he did. Reporting on the courts was a job for an experienced journalist, not a "cub," as young reporters are called; the job required knowledge of the system, and Steinbeck needed to cultivate inside sources, as well as develop a "nose" for telltale details that would point him toward a possible scandal. The old-timers did what they could to guide him in the right direction. "They pretended that I knew what I was doing," Steinbeck recalled years later, "and they did their best to teach me in a roundabout way." They even covered for him when he didn't show up for work, but all their kindness wasn't enough to save him in the end. Steinbeck was not discouraged, however, when the paper let him go. Instead, he told his friends he had reached a new level of accomplishment—he had been fired by a Hearst newspaper. At last, he said, he had some real credentials as a writer.

During these months in New York, Steinbeck fell in love for the second time. This time, the woman was Mary Ardath, a showgirl who performed in the Greenwich Village Follies. Mary was a beautiful young woman with green eyes and blond hair that she tied back with a ribbon. She was ambitious, and the idea of marriage to a down-and-out would-be novelist did not appeal to her. She tried to persuade Steinbeck to switch careers to something more lucrative and secure, like business, but he just laughed at her attempts to shape his future. Not surprisingly,

Steinbeck's romance with Mary lasted only a few weeks; Mary ultimately left a note telling him it was over. She married a banker soon thereafter, but years later, she had second thoughts about Steinbeck. She tracked him down to where he lived in California and showed up on his doorstep with her children. She had hoped they could pick up their relationship again, but because he was married by then, her hopes were dashed and she had missed her chance.

At the time of their initial breakup, many of Steinbeck's friends sided with Mary, and were critical of Steinbeck's stubbornness. Not only was Mary beautiful, but she had some money—she had been his meal ticket for weeks. One of Steinbeck's artist friends, Mahlon Blaine, felt particularly bad; he had hoped to have Mary as a free model for the rest of his life. But in spite of this disappointment, Blaine did all he could to help Steinbeck after he was fired from the newspaper. Blaine had an acquaintance, Guy Holt, who worked for the small publishing firm of Robert M. McBride & Company, and Blaine sent him some of Steinbeck's stories. Holt read the stories, and he liked them so much that he asked Steinbeck to come to his office for a meeting. "If you can write a half-dozen more stories of this quality," he said, "I'll publish a collection." The news excited Steinbeck, providing him with hope. He wrote frantically, putting together the stories Holt had requested, and after several weeks, he returned to McBride & Company with his collection, only to find that Holt had left to work for another publisher. The new editor was not interested in publishing any of Steinbeck's work, and refused to read the stories.

The pressure of the last few weeks, followed by this disappointment, was too much for Steinbeck. He fell apart, raging and threatening to tear the editor limb from limb. He went so far as to actually grab the man, but in the end, someone shoved him out of the office, down the stairs, and threw him out onto the sidewalk. His manuscript pages slipped from his grasp and floated out in a trail behind him. New York was proving to be too discouraging for the heartbroken Steinbeck, so he finally decided that his only option was to return to California.

He arrived back on the West Coast in the early summer of 1926. He visited his old Stanford roommate Dook Sheffield, and he even attempted (unsuccessfully) to re-kindle his romance with Margaret Gemmell. For what remained of the summer of 1926, Steinbeck worked again for Mrs. Price at Fallen Leaf Lake. While there, he met Mrs. Alice Brigham, the wealthy widow of a San Francisco surgeon who had a large summer home on the south shore of Lake Tahoe. She had heard good things about Steinbeck from Mrs. Price, and she offered him the job of caretaker at her Lake Tahoe home. He accepted the job, and finally, while he worked for Mrs. Brigham, Steinbeck had the solitude and time he needed to write, and he worked at the Lake Tahoe cottage for the better part of two years.

Busy Lake Tahoe turned into a ghost town in the winter, and Steinbeck, in the empty and lonely cottage, had a bit too much solitude on his hands. For the first time in his life, he was genuinely alone. But this isolation may have been exactly what he needed; it gave him the chance to realize that so long as he was always with other people, he would think about writing and talk about writing, but he would never get down to actually putting words on paper. During this time of isolation, then, he discovered that his artistic nature could only thrive in solitude. He found that whenever he listened to other people too much, he would end up distracted, depressed, and uncomfortable—and he would write nothing. During this time on Lake Tahoe, Steinbeck sold his first short story, "The Gifts of Iban," which was published in March, 1927, in *Smoker's Companion*. He also completed his first novel, *Cup of Gold*, at the beginning of 1928 (although the book was not published until a year and a half later).

PUBLICATION AND MARRIAGE

Cup of Gold stands apart from Steinbeck's other works, for unlike his better-known novels, which are realistic and tightly worded, *Cup of Gold* is a poetic fantasy, filled with metaphoric imagery. It tells the story of pirate Henry Morgan, and contains fantastical passages such as: "I imagine great dishes of purple porridge, drenched with dragon's milk, sugared with a sweetness only to be envisioned." Steinbeck's later characters, of course, would speak with a rough-edged brusqueness, but Henry Morgan recites long, melodramatic speeches:

> La Santa Roja ... has made cut-throats bay at the moon like lovesick dogs. She is making me crazy with vain desire. I must do something—anything—to lay the insistent haunting

of this woman I have never seen. I must destroy the ghost.
Ah, it is a foolish thing to dream of capturing the Cup of
Gold. It would seem that my desire is death.

Obviously, not many people talk like Henry Morgan. But although the
novel was pure fantasy, Steinbeck viewed the story as primarily
autobiographical. Henry Morgan's search for magic symbolized
Steinbeck's own search for his creative voice. He wrote to one of his
friends, "The book was an immature experiment written for the purpose
of getting ... all the autobiographical material (which hounds us until we
get it said) out of my system."

Cup of Gold earned Steinbeck little money. The small company that
published the book marketed it poorly, and many bookstores did not
carry it—those stores that did carry the book often mistook it for a
children's book because of the fantastical cover. Thus, in order to
support himself, Steinbeck was forced to work at more lucrative jobs
while he continued to write. To this end, he quit his job for Mrs.
Brigham, in the late spring of 1928, and began work at the Tahoe City
fish hatchery. He obtained this job through Lloyd Shebley, whom he had
met while living at Lake Tahoe. He and Shebley shared a bachelor
cottage behind the hatchery, and their work included cleaning duties,
feeding the newborn trout, and trapping the big lake trout when they ran
into a stream to spawn. They also had to take the eggs from the females
and put them where they could be fertilized by the males, and one day,
as Steinbeck was feeding ground liver to the fish, he mumbled, "I never
thought I'd be a midwife to a fish." Later, Shebley heard Steinbeck
hammering outside, and when he went out to look, he found that
Steinbeck had tacked a sign on the door of the private office that read:
PISCATORIAL OBSTETRICIAN.

At this time, between working and writing, Steinbeck dated a few
young women, but all of the relationships failed. In the summer of 1928,
however, while he was still working at the hatchery, he met a girl named
Carol Henning when she and her sister wandered in for a tour. Carol,
slightly younger than Steinbeck, was tall and slender with long brown
hair, and he was immediately attracted to her. The sisters stayed through
much of the afternoon, and when they finally had to go, Steinbeck asked
if he and Shebley could take the women out to dinner that night. Carol
was only in Tahoe for a 10-day vacation, but she spent all her time with

Steinbeck; when she left, he was miserable and began drinking heavily. His actions became so strange and violent during this time that his friends feared Steinbeck might be losing his mind.

But at summer's end, Lloyd Shebley left for Hollywood to pursue an acting career, and in September, Steinbeck lost his job at the hatchery and went to see Carol in San Francisco. There, his sister Mary's husband, Bill Dekker, got Steinbeck a job at the family's factory, the Bemis Bag Company. Steinbeck worked as a warehouseman, but again, he found it difficult to write when he was exhausted from physical work, and at the end of the year, Steinbeck quit his job and moved back to Pacific Grove. At Christmas, Steinbeck's father told his son that he had decided to let Steinbeck have the family's vacation house rent free; he would also loan Steinbeck $25 a month to live on while he pursued his writing. Steinbeck was to consider this as an advance against his future royalties, and Steinbeck was delighted and relieved by the proposition.

On New Year's Eve, Steinbeck and a friend went to San Francisco to visit Carol. The friend warned Carol not to marry Steinbeck, because, he said, she would never be as important to him as his writing. Carol was hurt; she cared as much about Steinbeck's writing career, she insisted, as Steinbeck did. And while he lived in Pacific Grove, Steinbeck worked on the manuscript of *The Green Lady*, which was published in 1933 under the title *To a God Unknown*. Carol visited him often during this time, but he wrote to a friend that he didn't think he would marry Carol, because he was afraid he wouldn't make her happy. "I would anger a wife," he wrote, "and then become angry because she was angry ... When I am working, I know that I am unbearable. So I guess marriage is not for me."

But there were other problems afoot. Even despite his father's support, Steinbeck's funds were short, as usual, so near the end of the following summer, he decided to go back to San Francisco to work just long enough to lay some cash aside to begin writing again. He also wanted to be closer to Carol, who was trying to talk him into marriage. She reminded him that he was a published author now, a success, well able to take on a wife, but Steinbeck knew he would need to publish many books before he could truly think of himself as successful. He worked part-time as a department store clerk, spending the rest of his time writing (when he wasn't with Carol). By the fall, Carol had argued away Steinbeck's doubts about marriage, and they announced their engagement to their families in November 1929.

His family was pleased, but Carol's family didn't like Steinbeck, and they liked him even less after he spent several days with them, when his car broke down near their home in San Jose. He was a tall, good-looking young man, but he was often moody and withdrawn, and he tended to sit alone, silent, a habit that made some people think he was "stuck up." At other times, of course, Steinbeck was an annoying showoff, and he also had a streak of pent-up violence that occasionally broke through to the surface, frightening those around him. As a result, Carol's parents had serious doubts about him as a future son-in-law.

Because the couple lacked Carol's parents' support, they were married in a small ceremony before a justice of the peace. Steinbeck's old college roommate Dook let them sleep in his living room, until Dook's wife became angry and kicked the couple out. They then took up residence in a "shanty" in the suburbs of Los Angeles. But the issue of income couldn't be staved off for long. Dook had received his master's degree from Stanford and taught at Occidental College; since Steinbeck was a published novelist, Dook assumed that Steinbeck should be able to land a teaching position as well. However, the plan didn't work out, mostly because Steinbeck refused to cooperate. So the Steinbecks repaired the shanty to make it look nice, but unfortunately, the owner of their house decided that the Steinbecks did such a good job, he would give the house to his daughter. Thus, Steinbeck and Carol had to search yet again for a new home.

The couple's next house was located within the Angeles National forest. Money was short, and the house was cheap. But after the Steinbecks had lived there a few weeks, they discovered that the rent was so low because the house was rumored to be haunted. Steinbeck claimed to have seen ghosts on previous occasions: a quiet, gracious ghost he encountered in Brooklyn, as well the gentlemanly ghost of Dr. Brigham, who would come to the door of Steinbeck's cabin on Lake Tahoe. But the ghost in Steinbeck's forest house was reportedly noisy and destructive. In the middle of the night, doors slammed; pictures fell off the walls; and dishes spun across the kitchen and broke on the other side of the room. These events fascinated Steinbeck, but the environment was far too disruptive for him to do any writing there. Carol looked for work, hoping that the added income would allow them to move into a new house, but she had no luck finding a job, and for the first time, the couple truly, personally understood the severity of the Great Depression.

The couple finally moved back to Steinbeck's family cottage in Pacific Grove, where they could live without paying rent. Their luck seemed to turn now as Carol landed a secretarial position in the Chamber of Commerce, and Steinbeck published an article in *Esquire*, describing his personal experience with the Great Depression. Also, to celebrate their marriage at this time, Steinbeck and Carol bought a puppy—a Belgian sheepdog called Oz (short for Ozymandias). Steinbeck had always loved dogs, and Oz was the first in a long line of canine companions (the most famous of them, of course, would be Charley, whom Steinbeck wrote about in his book, *Travels with Charley*).

And although Steinbeck's affection for dogs was certainly not uncommon, the author also possessed a sense of whimsy. One afternoon, for example, soon after Steinbeck and Carol married, Dook and his wife visited, and the wives both decided that they wanted to bleach their hair. One of them suggested testing the solution on Steinbeck's hair, which was normally dark and wavy. He agreed, and the women applied the peroxide and ammonia onto his scalp. Each application, however, turned his hair more pink, until it was the brilliant, flaming color of a sunset, streaked with rose and gold. To the women's dismay, Steinbeck was unbothered by this result. Carol pleaded with him to dye his hair back to normal, but he insisted he liked his hair being pink and gold and wanted to keep it that way. Several days later, the two couples went on a trip to the beach to visit Steinbeck's sister Mary, now married with children. Steinbeck drove a topless car, his wild, bright hair blowing in the wind. Other drivers stared at him, open-mouthed, and when they met Steinbeck's sister, she was so horrified by his appearance that she refused to speak to him. Meanwhile, her two children shrieked with laughter and tugged at his hair to see if it was real. But one week later, Steinbeck gave in and dyed his hair. However, instead of restoring it to its normal color, he had it dyed jet black, making it almost as dramatic and startling as his brilliant rose and gold hair had been.

Steinbeck maintained his mischievous good nature despite his financial hardships, yet he was forced to use his imagination to earn money. Desperate, he hurriedly wrote a mystery thriller called *Murder at Full Moon*. The story was about a man who went crazy every full moon, and a potbellied sleuth who looked like a potato bug and eventually tracks the villain down. Steinbeck wrote the story's 63,000 words in nine days, then submitted it under the pseudonym Peter Pym.

The mystery was never published—Steinbeck was so embarrassed by it that he eventually withdrew it in disgust—but it did put him in contact with a good New York agency, McIntosh & Otis, which would remain his agency to the end of his life. And while Steinbeck was pursuing these writing adventures, Carol and a group of her friends attempted to start up a plastics business. They had little success, but they had fun getting together trying to shape models out of a new Swiss plastic. The women called themselves the Faster Master Plaster Casters—Steinbeck watched from a distance, amused.

In the summer of 1932, Steinbeck's second novel, *The Pastures of Heaven* (actually a collection of interconnected short stories) was accepted for publication. Despite this news, however, the Steinbecks were still in fairly dire financial straits. They now lived in a little shack, roofed with tarpaper, in one of the poorer sections of Laguna Beach. Shortly after *Pastures of Heaven* appeared in bookstores, a young reporter from the weekly Laguna Beach Life came out to the Steinbecks' shack for an interview, wanting to ascertain Steinbeck's philosophy. Steinbeck remembered his own newspaper days, and how frustrated he had been when people didn't talk much during their interviews, so Steinbeck decided to give the interviewer something to write about. He began to plead wildly for the return of blood sacrifices, while the reporter stared at him in horror. Finally, she picked up her notebook and hurried off to write her story, anxious to tell the world that Steinbeck was a madman.

During these years, Steinbeck felt good about his marriage; Carol took care of him—she typed his manuscripts, encouraged him, cooked for him, and did his laundry, leaving him free to write. He felt guilty, however, as though he were tricking Carol; he didn't believe his work deserved such kingly treatment. His strict writing routine did little to help their marriage. Steinbeck would rise at seven o'clock, have a strong cup of coffee with Carol before she went off to her office, then go to his desk in the living room of the cottage, where he wrote until the middle of the afternoon. Then he would do a little gardening, and at four o'clock he would walk up to the headquarters of Pacific Biologicals, where he would talk to his friend Ed Ricketts. He would still be out when Carol came home from work, because he and Ed would usually eat dinner together and then spend some time in a bar. They might sit drinking until seven or eight at night, and sometimes he wouldn't come home until midnight. Justifiably, Carol often argued with Steinbeck about his routine.

Thus, Steinbeck's life in the late winter and spring of 1932 became a roller coaster. His writing was going well, he had more confidence than ever before, and he had supportive and creative close friends; but his relationship with Carol was strained. She was starved for attention, and Steinbeck seemed unable to give her the love she needed. He knew he was failing her, but he also, at this time, began to distrust her, paranoid that she would leave him for another man.

Meanwhile, on February 19, 1934, John's mother died of a stroke, brought on by high blood pressure. His father's health deteriorated rapidly after that, and a year later, he died of a brain hemorrhage.

At this time, in 1935, Steinbeck published a new novel, *Tortilla Flat*. Reflecting back on this time later, Steinbeck felt that his parents' deaths marked the end of the first part of his life; from this point on, he thought, he would be a successful author. But the days of poverty and fun, creativity and independence were over.

THE PRICE OF SUCCESS

Tortilla Flat earned Steinbeck his first taste of financial success, but he had mixed feelings about his newfound prosperity. Just a few months prior he had been wondering if he could even make it through the year without taking a job that paid a salary. Living close to the poverty line continually haunted him, and he was afraid this daemon might be essential to his writing. His writing, in part, had always sprung from his defiance of his parents' attitudes about money, and he worried that poverty was a necessary part of his creativity.

In April, 1936, Carol convinced Steinbeck to buy a piece of land about 50 miles north of Monterey, near Los Gatos, and build a house there. She wanted something that they owned themselves, rather than living in a house that had been a gift from the Steinbeck family, and she also hoped that she and her husband would be closer again if she had him to herself, away from some of his friends. In fact, the new house was so remote, it had neither electricity nor a telephone. Both Carol and Steinbeck, for their own separate reasons, liked the idea of being alone.

At this time, Steinbeck began work on *Of Mice and Men*, which later, of course, became his most popular novella. Originally, Steinbeck was going to call the work *Something That Happened*, thinking it would be a children's book, but the story strayed from his original plan. The changes may have come when Steinbeck was forced to re-write more than half of the book after his setter puppy destroyed a good chunk of the original manuscript.

In mid-August, 1936, George West, a young editorial writer from the San Francisco News, visited the Steinbecks. West admired Steinbeck's work, and although he doubted the famous novelist would be interested, he asked Steinbeck to write for his newspaper. Steinbeck liked the idea, and much to West's surprise, he accepted a commission to write a sequence of pieces about migrant farmers in California. He would visit various regions of the state to witness firsthand the conditions in which these people lived and worked. West was especially interested in the success or failure of the federal camps, because he had heard that many of the migrants there were undernourished and ill.

Steinbeck found that the migrant workers were frightened, desperate, and sinking deeper into debt as they tried, in vain, to find a way out of their situations. He talked with the father of a family of six who lived in a small tent, swarming with flies. Steinbeck watched while the family gathered to eat around an apple crate that served as their table; the meal consisted of fried dough, fried cornmeal, and beans— filling, but nutritionally inadequate. The mother did not have enough milk for her baby, and recently lost a child.

Another time, when Steinbeck offered one woman a cigarette, she took several puffs and vomited. Embarrassed, she apologized, explaining that the smoke made her sick because she hadn't eaten in two days. Steinbeck talked to another man who explained that his little girl couldn't go to school because she was too sick and weak to walk there. Every story Steinbeck heard made him realize more deeply the migrants' terrible poverty and hopelessness. From a distance, the migrants' camp looked like a city dump. The homes were built of anything and everything—scrap metal, flattened tin cans, burlap sacks, and corrugated cardboard, attached to branches driven into the ground. A single cold-water shower served 400 people, guards patrolled the camp with guns, and crowds were not allowed to gather, for fear they might organize into some sort of labor union; troublemakers were forced out of the camp at gunpoint.

Steinbeck found, however, that the government camps were better. At Weedpatch, a model government camp near Bakersfield, he met Tom Collins, a psychologist and government employee who was understanding and compassionate. Collins knew the camp's inhabitants and their problems, and he helped Steinbeck to understand their situation as well. At Weedpatch, the migrants could speak freely, with no fear of retaliation from the guards; in lieu of rent, they paid for their clean living quarters by devoting two hours a week to maintenance and camp improvement; food was sold at reasonable prices, and each family had a little plot of ground where they could raise their own vegetables. Steinbeck realized that these living conditions gave dignity back to the people.

Thus, while Steinbeck's own finances continued to improve, he could not forget the desperate poverty he witnessed at these camps. Eventually, he would put all he had learned from the migrants into his celebrated novel, *The Grapes of Wrath*; but at this time, Steinbeck published *Of Mice and Men* at the beginning of 1937, which proved an instant success. Letters arrived from strangers and friends alike, expressing their admiration for the book, and Steinbeck was swamped with requests for interviews, readings, public appearances, and autographs. During this time, Steinbeck learned that being famous could be a nuisance. Since he had no phone, he was often forced to travel several miles to the nearest one to respond to urgent requests of one kind or another. And once, a tourist turned up at his front gate with a young girl. When the woman saw Steinbeck, she had her daughter perform a dance for him, hoping to impress him. Steinbeck wrote to a friend, "This ballyhoo is driving me nuts."

Success was hard on Steinbecks' marriage, too. To get away from all the public attention, he and Carol took a trip to New York, but Steinbeck found that his fame preceded him there, and the couple's marital strain grew worse yet. After one particularly bad fight, Carol stormed off into the night, and when she didn't come back after several hours, Steinbeck checked hospitals and police stations. Carol returned the next morning, but Steinbeck was embarrassed and furious that their private problems had been exposed to the public. He became silent and withdrawn, and the more he withdrew into himself, the more wild and crazy Carol would act in public, hoping to get his attention. Their actions thus became a vicious circle; they each drove the other to the very behavior that the other hated most, and as a result, the emotional distance between them grew even greater. Soon, they decided to leave New York and board a freighter to vacation in Europe. On the first night at sea, they began to talk about the way they had each been acting, and while they traveled to Sweden, Denmark, Finland, Russia, and then back to New York, they were able to resolve their differences for the time being.

Fame brought other problems, though. Letters from destitute people often asked for handouts. One man asked for $100 to pay for his son's operation. "You got luck and I got no luck," the man wrote to Steinbeck. Carol wanted him to send this man the money, but Steinbeck refused. If he gave to one person, he said, he would have to give to everyone; how could he possibly choose who deserved his charity and who didn't? Such issues resurrected negative tension between Steinbeck and Carol.

For years, Carol shared Steinbeck's vision for his writing; she had helped him to clarify his thoughts by discussing his ideas with him endlessly; she had helped revise his manuscripts; she had typed his books; she had answered letters and phone calls for him; and all the while, she had kept house for him and made his life comfortable. Now, she felt left out and forgotten. She began to resent his success.

Despite their problems, Carol remained encouraging and supportive as Steinbeck began work on *The Grapes of Wrath*. While he wrote what would be considered his masterpiece, in August 1938, the couple bought a ranch on 50 acres of land, just north of Los Gatos. The new place had a swimming pool, a pond, woods, and was supposed to get them out of town and away from the public eye. The months that Steinbeck spent writing *The Grapes of Wrath* took a heavy physical toll on both him and Carol. Carol had to be hospitalized with a severe strep infection, and Steinbeck began to have sharp pains in his leg. He kept working until the book was done, however, and then collapsed. In January, 1939, medical tests showed that his metabolic rate was extremely low, indicating the presence of an infection somewhere in his body, and he was confined to his bed for two weeks. When rest failed to bring any improvement to the pain in his leg, he went back for more tests, and this time, x-rays showed two ulcers on the base of a tooth. It was extracted, and that seemed for a time to reduce the pain in his leg. But then the pain came back, and the leg continued to hurt him for most of that year. During that spring and summer, he was treated for tonsillitis, and his doctor removed his tonsils in July. Steinbeck slowly recovered, physically, but the wounds to his marriage did not heal as easily. His relationship with Carol fell apart all together, and they separated in 1941, their divorce finalized in 1943.

A RESTLESS MAN

Almost immediately following Steinbeck's separation from Carol, he fell in love again. His childhood friend Max Wagner, now an aspiring actor, introduced him to Gwyndolyn Conger, an aspiring actress and singer, and they became close at once. Gwyn was fascinated by Steinbeck and his work. She was twenty when they met, while Steinbeck was eighteen years her senior; yet despite the discrepancy in their ages, the two were married in New Orleans, in the home of one of Steinbeck's friends, on March 29, 1943.

When they returned to New York, though, Steinbeck learned he had been approved to go overseas as a war correspondent. The news upset Gwyn; being separated by an ocean did not seem like a good start for a marriage, and she tried everything she could to convince Steinbeck not to go. Gwyn grew disappointed and angry when she realized how little control she had over her new husband. Steinbeck nevertheless left for Europe in June and stayed until October, traveling around and reporting on whatever interested him. At the same time, his old interest in Arthurian legends sparked back to life, and he used his spare time for research. He had planned to write a book about Arthur one day, but although he never lost his interest in this subject, he never found the opportunity during his lifetime to write the book. His research on the subject was compiled and published posthumously.

On October 15, 1943, Steinbeck arrived back from Europe, physically and emotionally unwell. While away, he had seen things that had greatly upset him. At one point, he was near an explosion that left him with a twisted ankle, two blown eardrums, temporary memory loss, and recurring blackouts—though he didn't tell anyone about this last symptom until much later. Even more upsetting to him were the maimed children, and the atrocities he had witnessed; during this time, Steinbeck went into a state of prolonged shock. He was 41, and after reporting on the war from close range, he became obsessed with the idea that he was getting old; the thought of his own death haunted him. His blackouts reminded him of his mother's strokes, and he made himself even more unwell through constant worry. In addition, his relationship with Gwyn was of little comfort to him. She had retaliated against Steinbeck's decision to leave by trying to make him jealous, and Stienbeck thus became increasingly, painfully aware of their difference in age. He worried that he was too old to keep the interest of such a young wife, and he hated himself for being sick.

Gwyn, however, was also nervous and depressed. She had still not forgiven Steinbeck for leaving her so soon after their wedding, and her resentment served as the foundation for still more problems between them. Steinbeck seemed not to care that he had left her all alone in New York, terrified that he might be killed, and with no friends to comfort her. And now that he was back, he was a different man from the one she had married. He was thin and gray and sick, and she was unprepared for dealing with his moodiness. The funny, charming man she had met, and fell in love with, had disappeared.

In January, 1944, Steinbeck and Gwyn traveled by car to Mexico. It was a leisurely trip, and in Mexico, they enjoyed many foods, like steak, that were subject to the U.S. food rationing efforts. At this time, Steinbeck began to develop the idea for *The Pearl*. Soon, Gwyn became pregnant, with the baby due that summer. Upon reflection, Steinbeck decided he didn't want to raise a child in New York and thought that they should move back to Monterey. Gwyn, however, was developing a social life on the East Coast, and she bristled at the idea of moving back to small-town California. Finally, though, Steinbeck convinced Gwyn to move back west after the baby was born, and on August 2, Gwyn gave birth to a boy, Thom.

Two months later, Steinbeck drove across the country to California, while Gwyn and Thom followed him by airplane. When they arrived, they found that the house they had rented was too far away for them to be able to afford the gas they needed to drive into town—for gas too was rationed. They moved back, temporarily, to Steinbeck's parents' house in Pacific Grove, all the while looking for a place to buy. Steinbeck wanted an adobe house in the Carmel Valley, but the shortage of gasoline pushed the couple to look at houses closer to town. They ended up with an adobe home in town, where Steinbeck at least had enough room for a garden.

In February, 1945, Steinbeck and Gwyn traveled to Mexico again, for about a month, to work on the casting, locations, and music for the film version of *The Pearl*. They left Thom with Steinbeck's sister, Beth, and when they returned in the middle of March, they found their child big for his age—like his father was as a child—and their garden overflowing with produce: spinach, green onions, radishes, beets, lettuce, and carrots. "Things are shrieking they are growing so fast," Steinbeck wrote to a friend. He and Gwyn soon decided to have Thom baptized in the Episcopal Church. Neither of them was religious, but they thought Thom might need to be baptized; Steinbeck also thought that it wouldn't hurt for his son to absorb some of the language of the church.

Meanwhile, Monterey disappointed Steinbeck. He worried that his old friends avoided him; he could find no landlord willing to rent him office space; and the local gas board suddenly cut off his supply, claiming it was part of wartime rationing. A few weeks later, he was denied permission to continue the home repairs he had already begun, even though new homes were still being built. "I hate a feeling of persecution," Steinbeck wrote to a friend, "but I am just not welcome here." Beyond these external problems, Gwyn and Thom, in August 1945, developed a digestive illness, probably contracted in Mexico, and for Steinbeck, this was the final straw. He finally agreed with what Gwyn had felt all along: their return to Monterey had been a huge mistake, and their future lay in the East. California was no longer the place Steinbeck remembered, and Monterey rejected him.

In the middle of September, the Steinbecks bought two adjacent brownstones on East 78th Street in Manhattan, a secluded side street within easy reach of Midtown and a short stroll from Central Park. They had bought two houses because the residences shared a garden, and Steinbeck wanted to control this space as well as control who rented the place next to them.

In October, 1945, on his way to Mexico again to work on the filming of *The Pearl*, Steinbeck learned that Gwyn was pregnant again. He sent for her, but he was so involved with the filming that he did not have much time to spend with her. She felt left out and lonely, and after only three weeks, she flew back to New York, hurt and resentful. In addition, her second pregnancy was difficult, physically and emotionally—Gwyn felt miserable most of the time and constantly complained. When Steinbeck returned home, he spent most of his time looking after Thom. The Steinbecks' second son, John Steinbeck IV (later nicknamed "Catbird" by his father) arrived on June 12, 1946. The birth had been difficult, and Gwyn came home from the hospital exhausted. She went straight to bed, and for months, she remained there most of the day, suffering from a series of illnesses: flu, allergies, and fevers. Curious pains ran up and down her legs, and she claimed to have difficulty walking, but Steinbeck had little sympathy for her. He was suspicious of these recurring illnesses, concluding that they were mostly in Gwyn's mind, possibly even self-induced. Gwyn seemed sick all the time, and when she wasn't sick, she lacked energy and was unwilling to go anywhere, or do anything with him. In response, Steinbeck became moody and angry, and the two spent much of their time fighting.

Gwyn missed her career as a singer and hated housekeeping, and the marriage deteriorated further in the beginning of 1947. Gwyn left for California for some time, and after a month, Steinbeck flew out to join her. Their relationship apparently improved while they were on the West Coast, but when they returned to New York, their difficulties returned with them. To escape his tense marriage, Steinbeck decided to take a journalistic trip to Russia, but before he left, he had an accident at home. While he leaned over the second-story balcony to speak to a friend, the railing gave way, and Steinbeck fell. As he tumbled down, he reached out to protect himself from the spikes of the wrought-iron fence below. He managed to push away from them and land on his hands and knees, but he broke his kneecap and sprained his foot badly. He was bruised and scraped, and his knee required surgery. His trip to Russia had to be postponed for more than a month.

Eventually, however, Steinbeck did leave for Russia, and Gwyn travelled with him as far as France. Steinbeck continued on, with a photographer he had met in Europe during the war. Their trip lasted four months, and throughout this time, Steinbeck had to use a cane, bothered often by the pain in his knee and ankle.

When he returned, he decided he wanted to move back to California to research a new novel. Gwyn, for obvious reasons, did not like this idea and reminded Steinbeck of their last move. Gwyn's own career was starting to flourish, and she refused to be uprooted again simply because he couldn't settle down. Also, by this point, both children were active and lively, and even though the family had a full-time nursemaid, Gwyn felt that with her husband traveling so much, the burden of dealing with the children fell too much on her shoulders. Tellingly, at the end of the year, the family's nursemaid left for her vacation, and Gwyn fell ill again and stayed in bed most of the day. Steinbeck, tense and pressured as he struggled to finish his articles on Russia by their deadline, found himself having to take care of two small children; he grew frustrated, angry, and resentful. Friends commented later that Steinbeck would have done better if his boys could have been born 12 years old.

Desperate to escape from the pressures of his home life, Steinbeck decided to take a trip with his old friend from California, Ed Ricketts. The two men had made plans to travel to Canada's Queen Charlotte Islands when Steinbeck received word that Ricketts had been killed in a car-train accident. The news plunged Steinbeck into a terrible depression. His friend was dead, and shortly thereafter, Gwyn announced she wanted a divorce. Steinbeck packed several large suitcases—one full of various manuscripts in progress—kissed his children, and moved into a hotel suite.

At the beginning of September, 1948, Steinbeck moved back to Pacific Grove, California. Once there, he fell in love yet again, this time with a woman named Elaine Scott, who would become his third and last wife. Steinbeck and Elaine married in 1950, and after their wedding, they honeymooned in Bermuda, and then moved into a brownstone at 206 72nd Street, in New York City, where they lived for 13 years. Steinbeck's third marriage was thankfully happier and more stable, but he worried about his sons, especially Thom. Little John could take care of himself, but Thom always seemed sad and troubled, which hurt Steinbeck, but also made him identify with Thom. He confessed to a friend,

> I love him very dearly and I guess because of his faults which are my faults. I know where his pains and his panics come from. He can be ruined or made strong in this exact little time. And now is the time when I must help him—not by bolstering him up but by forcing here and making him learn to balance there.

Thom developed both emotional and learning problems, and Elaine tutored him on weekends and during the summer.

In 1952, Steinbeck finished *East of Eden*, another epic novel like *The Grapes of Wrath*. This book, however, merged Steinbeck's two styles of writing: the documentary-like factual account, and the romantic, allegorical storytelling that also attracted him. The book was based on the history of his own family, but it also included symbolism from the biblical story of Cain and Abel. When the book was done, Steinbeck and Elaine took a long trip to Europe, during which Steinbeck wrote some articles—he had been asked by *Colliers Magazine* to serve as a roving editor-at-large. The idea was not that he would do serious political reporting; rather, his commission was for personal pieces similar to those he had written during the war. He had established a reputation for being able to talk to ordinary people, and *Colliers* wanted him to seek people out, wherever fancy led him. His job was to make everyday events interesting, to find human stories and narrate them in his own way. By now, of course, American readers knew Steinbeck well, and they were familiar with his voice, and *Colliers* knew that because of Steinbeck's fame, anything he wrote would find an immediate audience, and Elaine, skilled with the camera, would take pictures to accompany the articles. In all, they were gone for six months, returning in time for the fall publication of *East of Eden*.

Steinbeck enjoyed the trip, but his pleasure was marred by the news that yet another friend had died, killed in an explosion. Once again, Steinbeck obsessed on the thought of his own inevitable death; his health deteriorated, and he sank into depression. But with the publication of *East of Eden*, Steinbeck developed a new interest: presidential candidate Adlai Stevenson. Steinbeck had liked Eisenhower as a general, but when he heard Stevenson's speeches, Steinbeck decided to support Stevenson for president instead of Eisenhower, and for the rest of his life, he described his politics by saying he was a "Stevenson Democrat." He liked Stevenson's sense of humor and honesty, as well as his refreshing lack of slogans, and when Stevenson's supporters learned of Steinbeck's admiration for the candidate, they asked him to write the forward to a collection of Stevenson's speeches, published as part of his campaign. In the foreword, Steinbeck wrote, "I think Stevenson is more durable, socially, politically and morally ... As a writer I love the clear, clean writing of Stevenson. As a man I like his intelligent, humorous, logical, civilized mind." Needless to say, Steinbeck was deeply disappointed when Stevenson lost to Eisenhower.

In the spring of 1954, the Steinbecks took another trip to Europe, traveling by boat to Spain, and buying a Jaguar to drive while on the

Continent. Before they had left home, though, Steinbeck applied for life insurance, and while in Spain, he learned that he had been turned down. The doctor who examined him had discovered that he had abnormally small heart, which meant it would have to work unusually hard to keep his large body functioning. Steinbeck, horrified, decided to go to a specialist in Paris, but before he could get to the appointment, he suffered an attack of some kind, either heart failure or a small stroke—perhaps brought on by the stress of finding that some of his fears about his health had been confirmed.

Steinbeck and Elaine rented a house in Paris, and under the specialist's care, his health improved. During the summer, his sons, Thom and John, visited them, and then, through the fall, Steinbeck and Elaine traveled around Europe once again—to England, Greece, and Italy. As always, Steinbeck was too restless to stay in one place for very long, and they returned to New York just before Christmas.

In February, 1955, the Steinbecks bought a house in Sag Harbor on Long Island, though they did not spend all their time there. Instead, they spent the following year working hard, once again, to get Adlai Stevenson elected, and during this campaign, Steinbeck became involved in speech-writing. But of course, to Steinbeck's great disappointment, Stevenson lost again.

In late 1956, Steinbeck joined a program called People to People, which the Eisenhower administration had organized. The idea behind the program was to have certain prominent people in the United States make contact with private citizens and prominent people in countries behind the Iron Curtain. (This was the term Winston Churchill had given to the boundary around Soviet-controlled lands.) This occurred at the height of the Cold War, when Russia and the U.S. were at odds with one another without ever actually declaring war, and Steinbeck, though somewhat reluctantly, joined the writers' committee of People to People, chaired by William Faulkner. (Other writers on the committee included Edna Ferber, William Carlos Williams, Donald Hall, Robert Hillyer, and Saul Bellow.) As a part of this committee, Steinbeck was eager to discuss why the United States had failed to send aid to refugees after the Russian invasion of Hungary, among other issues. Steinbeck had strong political beliefs, but the committee had few tangible results; the one thing it did accomplish had nothing at all to do with the Cold War.

The poet Ezra Pound had been convicted of treason for giving aid and support to the enemy while he lived in Italy during World War II, but instead of jail or execution, he had been put into St. Elizabeth's mental hospital in Washington. Urged on by Donald Hall, the writers' committee of People to People put together a proposal to free Pound from his imprisonment. Steinbeck, surprisingly, argued against this idea; he believed it would anger the American public and hurt the committee's influence, but Faulkner insisted, and Pound was eventually released.

These were troubled days in America's history. The threat of communism seemed real and frightening, and people looked at each other with suspicion, wondering who secretly sympathized with the enemy. Those who had radical ideas were not trusted, and Steinbeck, who had always felt deeply about the rights of human beings, had never learned the art of tact, offending people more often than not. He continued to write with the same discipline he had learned while writing *The Grapes of Wrath*, but his restlessness continued to drive him from one journey to the next, and when he was not traveling, he frequently moved to a new home, as though he thought that somewhere, some place, he would find the answer to his life's dilemmas. As his health deteriorated, however, he began to realize he needed to find a quiet, stable place where he could retreat. As he had learned so long ago when he worked in the empty resort on Lake Tahoe, his writing required that he make a place for himself where he could be undisturbed by other people. Here, in this quiet place, he decided, he would retire.

THE FINAL YEARS

On the property at Sag Harbor, Steinbeck built a little workroom at the end of a point of land. At first, he joked that he would call his retreat "Sanity's Stepchild," but eventually he named it "Joyous Garde," after the castle where Lancelot took Guinevere. Steinbeck was still fascinated with the Arthurian legends, just as he had been when he was a boy, and he identified most with Lancelot. With this in mind, he put a sign over the door of his new workroom, hand-inscribed in old English, and moved in, delighted to at last have a place he could go to escape from the noise and chaos of his life. He had made the room small enough so that only one seat would fit comfortably in the center; that way, if anyone did happen to wander out to visit him, the visitor would have no place to sit down. The seat, a director's chair with "Siege Perilous" lettered on the canvas back (another reference to the Arthurian legends), was nearly surrounded by a desk and countertop, so that John could spread out papers and books in all directions. He put a bookshelf all around the room over the windows, and he had a hot plate, an intercom, an electric pencil sharpener, and his adjustable drafting table with an adjustable fluorescent light. This was Steinbeck's idea of heaven. And though he may have thought of himself as retired, he did not stop writing, nor did he stop his restless travels around the world. But as the 1950s drew to a close, Steinbeck had definitely slowed down.

Late in the fall of 1959, Elaine was working in the kitchen when she smelled something burning. She rushed up to the third floor, where Steinbeck had been reading in his bedroom, and found him unconscious and smoldering. He had dropped a cigarette in the bed and set fire to the sheets and his pajamas, but Elaine managed to put the fire out and called an ambulance. Apparently, John had suffered another small attack of some sort, just as he had in Paris.

Nevertheless, in the spring of 1960, he began planning a cross-country trip. He wanted to relearn the taste of his own country, he told friends. Filled with excitement, he wrote:

> I'm buying a pickup truck with a small apartment on it kind of like the cabin of a small boat, bed, stove, desk, ice-box, toilet—not a trailer—what's called a coach. I'm going alone, out toward the West by the northern way but zigzagging through the Middle West and the mountain states. I'll avoid cities, small towns and farms and ranches, sit in bars and hamburger stands and on Sunday go to church. I'll go down the coast from Washington and Oregon and then back through the Southwest and South and up the East Coast but always zigzagging. Elaine will join me occasionally but mostly I have to go alone, and I shall go unknown. I just want to look and listen. What I'll get I need badly—a re-knowledge of my own country, of its speeches, its views, its attitudes and its changes. It's long overdue—very long.

Steinbeck left for his trip on September 23, 1960. He brought his dog with him, and he described their adventures in his book, *Travels with*

Charley. The book had a cheerful tone, but in reality, Steinbeck was disturbed by what he found on his trip. Most Americans, he discovered, didn't have any real opinions; all they cared about was sports and hunting. He was especially upset by the racism he found in the South, and so he completed the journey in only 11 weeks, rushing rather than lingering along his way as he had originally planned.

On a trip to Europe, in the fall of 1961, Steinbeck suffered another heart attack (or small stroke) while in a hotel in Milan. He recovered quickly, however, and on Christmas Eve he had an audience with Pope John XXIII, along with about twenty other people.

The following year—specifically October, 1962—Steinbeck received word that he had been awarded the Nobel Prize for Literature. The announcement aroused mixed reactions among the public, however; many Americans did not think Steinbeck deserved the prize, so instead of bringing him greater fame, the Nobel Prize was increasingly dismissed by many critics. Nevertheless, in the early spring of 1963, President Kennedy asked Steinbeck to visit the Soviet Union as part of a cultural exchange program, designed to diminish the tensions of the Cold War. However, the trip had to be postponed for several months when Steinbeck woke up one morning, unable to see out of one eye. He needed an immediate operation for a detached retina, and he was forced to lie in bed for weeks, blindfolded and immobilized by sandbags designed to prevent him from moving his head.

In late September of that year, fully recovered at last from eye surgery, Steinbeck flew with Elaine to Washington for a briefing at the State Department. When he met with the President, he said, "I hope you don't mind if I kick up some dirt while I'm there?" Kennedy laughed and said, "I expect you to." The Steinbecks had traveled around Eastern Europe and the Soviet Union for a month, and were visiting Warsaw, when they learned of Kennedy's assassination. Horrified, Steinbeck decided he could no longer continue with his mission, and that he needed time to mourn. The State Department suggested that the couple go to Vienna, where a funeral service for Kennedy was held at a cathedral, and then they returned home in the middle of December.

But for Steinbeck, the bad news continued when in 1965, his favorite sister, Mary, died. Elaine later remarked that "each death seemed to take a little more out of him." At the time, Steinbeck was overwhelmed by "the feeling that everyone he loved was leaving him."

He continued writing, and in 1966, *America and Americans*, a series of essays accompanied by photos, was published, after which *Newsday* suggested that Steinbeck go to Vietnam as a correspondent. His son, John, now a young man, had been sent to Vietnam, and Steinbeck had been wanting to visit the country ever since. He did not want to go as part of a political mission, as Lyndon Johnson's emissary, but he had wanted to go independently, and *Newsday*'s offer was the perfect opportunity. Steinbeck brought Elaine with him, proud that she would go anywhere and try anything. "I am not going places any more without Elaine," he wrote to a friend. "Life is too short to be away from her."

The trip caused Vietnam to become the topic that dominated Steinbeck's writing during the last years of his life. His reactions to the war followed a curve: at first, he doubted whether the United States should be involved; then, he moved toward strong support of American policy, and was particularly outspoken in his defense of the integrity of U.S. troops in Vietnam; and finally, he returned once more to his original doubts about the wisdom of American participation. During this controversial era, many young Americans felt that U.S. involvement in the fighting was immoral, but Steinbeck, for all his doubts, never felt that the Vietnam War was wrong any more than, in his opinion, all war was wrong. He believed that the American government's actions were inspired by idealism—a belief in freedom for all people—even if this idealism was misguided.

Furthermore, Steinbeck saw in American soldiers the same kind of nobility, born out of adversity, that he had once witnessed in the Okies from the Midwest Dust Bowl. These soldiers were fighting for the survival of others and for human dignity against those who would take it away. Furthermore, they were doing so within a hostile environment, against a brutal and totally ruthless enemy. They had many restrictions on how they could fight, and they lacked support and appreciation from home. Thus, like the characters in Steinbeck's novels of the 1930s, American soldiers were both victims and heroes—victims because they were ordinary people caught in a mess beyond their control, a mess that made others look down on them, just as people had once looked down on the Okies; and heroes because, in the face of terrible discouragement, these soldiers were capable of great courage and sacrifice. Steinbeck might have turned against the war, but he never turned against the men fighting it.

Steinbeck was a loyal father, as he demonstrated in 1967, when his son, John, was charged with possession of marijuana; twenty pounds of which were found in his room. When John went to confront Steinbeck, he found his father lying flat on his back, immobilized from back surgery, but with his mind as active as ever. At that time, Steinbeck devoted all his mental energies toward thinking of ways to help his son out of the mess he was in. Young John must have hidden a smile when he saw his father, for he was an odd sight, head propped up on pillows, wearing a W. C. Fields T-shirt, and a stuffed canary perched on the bridge of his glasses that seemed to be reading the book in his lap. On the wall was a poster that read, SMOKE PEANUT BUTTER, NOT POT. As it turned out, the drugs had belonged to someone else, and John IV was acquitted a few months later.

Though Steinbeck eventually recovered from his surgery, he was never really well again. He and Elaine moved back to New York City from Sag Harbor in order to be closer to hospitals and doctors, as Steinbeck's medical condition was rapidly worsening.

On Memorial Day weekend in 1968, Steinbeck had another small stroke, and in July, during a heat wave, he had a small heart attack. In November, he experienced trouble breathing, and suffered the onset of emphysema. Finally, on the afternoon of December 20, 1968, John Steinbeck died. Elaine printed an announcement in the papers requesting that no flowers be sent, yet flowers came from all over the world, honoring the author who had cared so passionately about those who suffered from injustice. For all his personal faults, Steinbeck had produced a lifetime of writing that reflected his unique compassion and social consciousness, and after his death, several more of his incomplete works were published posthumously. Ultimately, his books would continue to inspire readers for generations to come.

At Steinbeck's funeral, in New York City, Henry Fonda, the actor, read some of Steinbeck's favorite poems, and then, on the afternoon before Christmas, Elaine and Thom took John's ashes to California. For two nights, the silver box rested in the garden of the family house in Pacific Grove, and after Christmas, Steinbeck's sisters arranged a small, private funeral service on Point Lobos, on a cliff overlooking Whaler's Bay, a spot Steinbeck and his sister Mary had loved when they were children. A priest presided over the service, then took a handful of ashes and released them in the wind. Steinbeck's family watched an otter play in the sea below, and a gull cried out as it circled the sky. To Steinbeck's family, it seemed that the writer's restless spirit was finally, truly free at last.

MICHAEL PRICE

Champion of the Common Man: John Steinbeck and His Achievement

Because 2002 marked the centennial of John Steinbeck's birth, a renaissance of public interest in, and scholarship on the writer is now taking place, thus providing many opportunities to reflect on Steinbeck's achievements. But what about Steinbeck's art is praiseworthy, and what is not? What are his major contributions to American literary history? What characterizes his writing? What themes, ideas, and symbols, appear and reappear in his work? In short, what elements combine to make a work quintessential to this writer? Such questions should not only motivate us to read, or reread, Steinbeck's work, but should also bring us to a more comprehensive understanding of it.

Steinbeck's body of work as a whole (i.e., his corpus) reveals the scope and magnitude of his achievement. The sheer depth and breadth, not to mention the quality, of Steinbeck's corpus is a stunning achievement, indeed. But what can be learned by envisioning Steinbeck's writings as a whole? Certainly, patterns emerge that link the man, and how he lived, to his art.

STEINBECK'S WORK ETHIC

When you pick up a Steinbeck book, of course, you handle the finished product. But what happened behind the scenes? Reflecting upon Steinbeck as a young man and artist, one of his friends recalled, "In all my life ... I've never known anyone else to concentrate more deeply on writing or work so hard at writing as John" (Timmerman, 3). Steinbeck strained every nerve and fiber of his being to produce his books, spending countless hours at his desk writing and then rewriting. He once remarked that "three hours of writing require twenty hours of preparation" (15), and reportedly, he practiced what he preached. To cite just a few examples, he rewrote his 1962 Nobel Prize acceptance speech "at least" twenty times (4); rewrote *Cup of Gold* six times; and *The Grapes of Wrath* required a decade of germination for Steinbeck.

In addition, Steinbeck demonstrated great determination as he strove to avoid complacency. When he sensed that he was growing stale, he often took drastic measures to re-energize himself (as *Travels With Charley*—a book undertaken when Steinbeck decided to drive with only his dog cross-country, talking to ordinary citizens—illustrates). His ethic also manifested itself by way of his ceaseless attempts at experimentation, including his invention of, and work toward, a hybrid genre called the play-novelette, which required refashioning a play into a novella, or vice-versa. He also invented, and skillfully applied, a narrative device called the "interchapter," or "intercalary chapter," which certainly, as a form, contributed to the achievement of a new, and distinct, novel structure in both *The Grapes of Wrath* and *East of Eden*. Steinbeck considered the writing process itself so compelling, in fact, that he meditated upon it often in his letters and his journals.

STEINBECK'S NON-FICTION

Steinbeck is famous primarily—perhaps justifiably—for his fiction, but he also wrote and published a considerable body of non-fiction work, including writings in such disparate genres as: investigative journalism, travelogues, essays, letters, journals, World War II articles, and documentary material (later used in screenplays for both *The Forgotten Village* and *Viva Zapata!*). For this reason, Steinbeck's image as writer is rendered at best incomplete—at worst distorted—when readers fail to factor in his non-fiction work, and thus neglect a significant portion of Steinbeck's artistic output.

STEINBECK'S SETTINGS

Steinbeck tended to set his early stories in two places: the Salinas Valley, inhabited by hard-working farmers, ranchers, and migrant workers; and the region where Steinbeck grew up, or Monterey, the seaside community populated by loafers, blindly-ambitious careerists, and assorted others. Steinbeck used these two locales as the backdrop for his two collections of short stories, *The Pastures of Heaven* and *The Long Valley*, and many of his novels. But as Steinbeck became more successful, and therefore more prosperous, he traveled extensively and established residences outside California, and soon, the characters in some of his works seemed to follow, also living and working in non-California locales. Some critics believe, however, that Steinbeck's self-imposed exodus from his home state proved harmful: "The further Steinbeck moved from this spring of personal experience that nourished his work, the less successful his work was" (Timmerman, 211).

Steinbeck, too, ultimately came to believe that leaving his home state benefited neither him nor his writing. In fact, in 1960, as he was preparing to embark on the cross-country journey that would result in the travelogue, *Travels With Charley: In Search of America*, Steinbeck realized that he had lost touch with his home, central California, and that it was time to rediscover both himself and his country:

> For many years I have traveled in many parts of the world. In America I live in New York, or dip into Chicago or San Francisco. But New York is no more America than Paris is France or London is England. Thus I discovered that I did not know my own country. I, an American writer, writing about America, was working from memory, and the memory is at best a faulty, warpy reservoir. I had not heard the speech of America, smelled the grass and trees and sewage, seen its hills and water, its color and quality of light. I knew the changes only from books and newspapers. But more than this, I had not felt the country for twenty-five years. In short, I was writing of something I did not know about ... So it was that I determined to look again, to try to rediscover this monster land.

To this end, Steinbeck outfitted a pick-up truck with a camper, christened it "Rocinante" (named after Don Quixote's horse), and crossed the country, mainly via back roads. Not surprisingly, Steinbeck often equated his own sense of identity with his sense of place—a quintessentially American perspective.

STEINBECK ON STAGE

Steinbeck not only wrote for the stage, he invented a hybrid genre for it: the play-novelette. This consists of a work that can, with minimal refashioning, function as a play or a novella. Usually, Steinbeck made this possible by placing the action in a few central locations, intensifying and focusing the story's conflict, and stressing the dialogue (conveniently, one of his literary strong suits). *Of Mice and Men*, his first experiment in this genre, was a smash hit: it ran for 207 performances in New York City and won the New York Drama Critics' Circle Award as the best play of the year. Critic Robert Morsberger noted, "Reviews ranged from enthusiastic to ecstatic" (Morsberger, 276). A testament to its timelessness, *Of Mice and Men* is still regularly revived, even to the extent that it "has attained the stature of a dramatic classic" (277).

However, Steinbeck's second venture into the play-novelette, *The Moon is Down*, did not fare as well. Its story concerns the way a small, Norwegian town resisted the German forces that invaded and occupied it. And though the story is compelling, the play-novelette was bedeviled by two problems. First, Steinbeck finished the play version on December 7, 1941, the start of America's involvement in World War II. Second, many critics felt that during wartime—especially in 1942, when the Allies were, in many places, losing the war—Steinbeck erred by portraying the invading force as too human, too sympathetic. Nevertheless, the novella version, which appeared in March, 1942, sold almost one million copies in that year alone and has since been hailed, arguably, as "the best World War II novel written during the war" (Morsberger 279). And the play did, in fact, place second in the New York Drama Critics' voting for the best play of the year, though it ran for only 9 weeks on Broadway.

It was better received on the road, though, particularly in London and Stockholm, where, in 1943, it was "a smash hit" (Morsberger, 283). In these locales and others, *The Moon is Down* resonated with so much power that the King of Norway "decorated Steinbeck for the support that both novel and play gave the resistance movement" (283). Elsewhere, the Germans, upset by the play's content, drove the play-novelette underground and put to death anyone caught possessing it (283). Tellingly, *The Moon is Down* has been translated into eighty languages, thus demonstrating the widespread interest that the work generated, despite its theatrical failure in America.

Steinbeck's third play-novelette, *Burning Bright*, is "generally considered Steinbeck's poorest work" in his entire corpus (Morsberger, 271). Though the play was produced by musical theater icons Rogers and Hammerstein, both it, and the novella version, failed miserably. Nonetheless, however, this was not the last of Steinbeck's collaborations with Rogers and Hammerstein, who later adapted Steinbeck's novel *Sweet Thursday* into an unmemorable musical entitled "Pipe Dream."[1]

In short, although Steinbeck's achievement in theater comprised a mixed bag, his work and experimentation in this arena must be included and considered when taking stock of his body of work, as should his role in film production.

STEINBECK ON SCREEN

Unlike F. Scott Fitzgerald, William Faulkner, or Ernest Hemingway—contemporaries who also involved themselves in Hollywood productions—Steinbeck had great successes on the big screen. As Robert Morseberger noted, "most Steinbeck films have been both artistic and commercial successes, and a number of them [such as *Of Mice and Men* and *The Grapes of Wrath*] have become screen classics." Indeed, over the course of his career, Steinbeck was three times nominated for the screenwriting Academy Award, while his films, more generally, garnered twenty-five Academy Award nominations, ultimately winning four (Morseberger, 339).

Among the dozen or so of Steinbeck's film credits, one can find three categories of films: films written by Steinbeck; films Steinbeck adapted from his own fiction; and films others adapted from Steinbeck's fiction. Critic Robert Morsberger's compilation of credits for these films is a testament to their quality (Zapata, 361-365): the first film version of *Of Mice and Men* starred Burgess Meredith as George and Lon Chaney, Jr., as Lennie, with a musical score by Aaron Copland; the original

version of *The Grapes of Wrath*, which became a classic, stars Henry
Fonda as Tom Joad; *Tortilla Flat* starred Spencer Tracy as Pilon; Elia
Kazan directed, and James Dean starred, in *East of Eden*; Jayne Mansfield
starred as Camille in *The Wayward Bus*; and Alfred Hitchcock produced
and directed the Steinbeck-penned *Lifeboat*.[2]

Steinbeck's towering achievement in film is most embodied by
Viva Zapata!, a film Morseberger regards as "unquestionably his finest
work in the genre" (Morseberger, 348). Steinbeck wrote the screenplay
for *Viva Zapata!*, which was directed by Elia Kazan, and a young, twenty-
eight year old Marlon Brando played the lead role. Emiliano Zapata, the
movie's subject, was a Mexican farmer who, when thrust into the
Mexican Civil War (which began in 1910), emerged as a "born leader
and military genius," serving with rare distinction until his assassination
in 1919 (3). Zapata was a serendipitous subject choice for Steinbeck, who
had studied him for twenty years, but initially, Steinbeck's thorough
knowledge of the man was a handicap. That is, the first draft of the *Viva
Zapata!* screenplay was so scholarly that it resembled a Ph.D.
dissertation; Hollywood, however, wanted a filmscript. Steinbeck
accordingly returned to his desk, and revised the manuscript; once the
film was released, *Viva Zapata!* electrified audiences. It earned Steinbeck
an Academy Award nomination for best story and screenplay; Marlon
Brando earned an Oscar nomination for best actor, while Anthony
Quinn actually won the Oscar for best supporting actor. Indeed, Robert
Morseberger ranks *Viva Zapata!* as one of the four "most memorable
films of 1952," placing it in the elite company of *High Noon*, *Singin' in
the Rain*, and *The Quiet Man* (Morseberger, 15).

Even after Steinbeck's death, his works continued to attract
Hollywood attention. There were productions—or, in some cases,
remakes—of *Cannery Row*, *The Chrysanthemums*, *The Raid*, *Molly Morgan*
(from *The Pastures of Heaven*), and *Of Mice and Men*, to name a few.
Steinbeck's works were also posthumously adapted for television,
including *Of Mice and Men*, *The Red Pony*, *East of Eden*, and *The Winter of
Our Discontent*. *Of Mice and Men*, in fact, was remade twice: the 1968
version starred George Segal and Nicol Williamson as George and
Lennie; the 1981 version, Robert Blake and Randy Quaid (Morsberger,
356). *East of Eden* was made into a four-hour television miniseries, and
the 1983 production of *The Winter of Our Discontent* starred Donald
Sutherland and Teri Garr.

STEINBECK, MEXICO, AND KING ARTHUR

Growing up in the Salinas Valley of California, Steinbeck for years had "lived near, worked with, and studied the Mexicans and their culture" (Shillinglaw, 1084). He accepted and sympathized with them—as he often did with societal "underdogs"—and displayed none of the contempt for so-called "wetbacks" that many Americans harbored. For instance, when Elia Kazan approached Steinbeck in 1952 to ask whether Steinbeck would be interested in writing a screenplay about Emiliano Zapata, a hero in the Mexican Civil War, Steinbeck replied that he had already been thinking of Zapata for the preceding twenty years—since the publication of his first novel. Compelled by his own curiosity, in the early 1930's, Steinbeck—who was fluent in Spanish—began taking trips to Mexico to compile an oral history of Zapata. His research continued in 1940, when he visited Mexico on his sea voyage with Ed Ricketts (recounted in *The Sea of Cortez*), and later, when he visited to write the screenplay for a documentary entitled *The Forgotten Village*, which told the story of rural Mexican Indians who, while suffering an epidemic, refused to be treated with modern medicine. While there on that assignment, Steinbeck continued to gather information on Zapata, and at that time, he began to supplement oral histories with material from a handful of books that were then available about Zapata. Though this project was often, necessarily, on the back burner for Steinbeck, his research re-gained momentum in the late 1940's, when he again had many opportunities to travel to Mexico, and spent significant amounts of time there.

By autumn 1949, Steinbeck had completed what he believed to be the screenplay (called *Zapata, the Little Tiger*), but as mentioned before, the tome was so overwhelmingly comprehensive and scholarly that it seemed fit for the ivory towers of academia rather than a Hollywood production that Steinbeck had to revise and rethink the whole script. Thus, when *Viva Zapata!* finally appeared on screen in 1952, it was the culmination of not only twenty years of study, but also Steinbeck's apprenticeship in writing for Hollywood. Of course, during that same span of time—while Steinbeck studied Zapata and Mexico—Steinbeck mulled over the "American" material that would go into his works of the 1930's and 1940's. Correlations in Steinbeck's work, understandably, evolved then between the "American" and "Mexican" material, such as an overriding sympathy for poor, dispossessed farmers from both nations.

Between 1929 and 1962, Steinbeck composed twenty works of fiction, in various forms; approximately half of these works involve Mexicans. (Seven feature Mexican-Americans, while three focus on Mexicans in Mexico.) Furthermore, in the seven works featuring Mexican-Americans, Steinbeck identifies approximately sixty of them by name, with the highest number appearing in *Tortilla Flat* (Metzger, 141). The prevalence, as well as prominence, of Mexican culture confers upon Steinbeck's work an atmosphere, or a way of life, more appealing than that of "respectable" middle-class, career-seeking whites. But what is that "certain something" Steinbeck captured and preserved?

Arthur F. Kinney identified one aspect of it: the pervasive presence of Sir Thomas Malory's King Arthur cycles. In *Tortilla Flat*, for example, Steinbeck portrays Mexican-American characters (or "paisanos") in terms of King Arthur and the Knights of the Round Table. Viewing the paisanos in this context, Danny parallels King Arthur, while Danny's friends resemble the Knights of the Round Table. Their loyalty to Danny, and to one another, recalls the unbreakable bond—the *comitatus*—that links Arthur to his knights, and in a mock-heroic way, their escapades parallel those of the Knights of the Round Table. Indeed, near the end of *Tortilla Flat*, when Danny runs wild for weeks, his recklessness is likened to Sir Lancelot's madness. Plus, the paisanos search for the Holy Grail, which, in their case, ends anticlimactically when they just find a landmarker for a 1915 "geodetic survey" (Kinney, 40). And just as Arthur's knights disband when Arthur dies, so Danny's friends disperse after Danny dies. Kinney cites multiple parallels, concluding that:

> in developing a comic tone, a mock-epic development, Steinbeck at once keeps close to his reader the Arthurian cycle, while he himself remains a good step in aesthetic distance from it ... The result, therefore, is a successful transposition of the legend. Steinbeck avoided the dangers of too close a parallel. At the same time, he used the advantages inherent in choosing a legend for modern treatment. In forging such a middle road between the danger and the advantage, he turned a possibility into a profit, treacherous

going into triumph: *Tortilla Flat* is quite possibly the best Arthurian story for which a modern society can serve as basis (Kinney, 46).

Charles Metzger, among others, has argued that the paisanos from *Tortilla Flat* are reincarnated as the wino-bums who inhabit Monterey in *Cannery Row* and *Sweet Thursday*, but outside of Monterey, Mexicans appear even more frequently in Steinbeck's work. Twelve Mexican-Americans appear in *To a God Unknown*, and some also appear in Steinbeck's short stories. For example, bad fortune befalls Pepe Torres in "Flight" (from *The Long Valley*) and the Gitano in "The Great Mountains" (from *The Red Pony*). Conversely, the protagonist of *The Wayward Bus*, Juan Chicoy, is portrayed as a kind of hero, a "muy hombre" (Metzger, 152). Metzger goes so far as "to suggest that there is possibly no other character in his fiction ... that Steinbeck appears to admire more openly than he does Juan Chicoy" (153). But Steinbeck also glorifies a Mexican-American man named "Joseph and Mary Rivas" (two names, yet one person), who appears in *Sweet Thursday* as the counterpart to Doc. Metzger elaborates: "the idealistic Joseph and Mary is ... presented as an admirable, colorful, romantic character. He is handsome, intelligent, and friendly ... He is a logical development of the rogue hero" heretofore illustrated by Danny and Juan Chicoy (154).

Obviously, in addition to consistently positive portrayals of Mexicans and Mexican-Americans, an Arthurian subtext undergirds and informs *Tortilla Flat*, *Cannery Row*, and *Sweet Thursday*—works that span the beginning, middle, and end of Steinbeck's career. But this discovery merely scratches the surface of a lifelong obsession. Steinbeck had always been fascinated with the Arthurian legends after being first introduced to Malory's *Morte D'Arthur* as a child. "A passionate love for the English language opened to me from this one book," he wrote (Metzger, 4). Like Steinbeck's affinity for Mexico and its people, the Arthurian literature Steinbeck loved so much wended its way often into his own work. Besides *Tortilla Flat*, *Cannery Row*, and *Sweet Thursday*, Arthurian legend seeps into *Cup of Gold*, Steinbeck's first novel; one character is named "Merlin," and the protagonist seeks "the cup of Gold."

More importantly, though, during the sixteen years between 1952 and Steinbeck's death in 1968, much of his time and energy was devoted to "researching and translating Malory's *Morte D'Arthur*" (Shillinglaw, 1087), and eventually, his labors bore fruit: his own version, entitled *The Acts of King Arthur and His Noble Knights*, was published in 1976. The work consists of seven stories: "Merlin," "The Knight With Two Swords," "The Wedding of King Arthur," "The Death of Merlin," "Morgan Le Fay," "Gawain, Ewain, and Marhalt," and "The Noble Tale of Sir Lancelot of the Lake." But what motivated Steinbeck to undertake such a project? Certainly it was, at least in part, a labor of love, but there was more to it. Steinbeck wanted to leave something for his children:

> I wanted to set them [the legends] down in plain, present-day speech for my own young sons, and for other sons not so young—to set the stories down in meaning as they were written, leaving out nothing and adding nothing—perhaps to compete with the moving pictures, the comic-strip travesties which are the only available source for those children and others of today who are impatient with the difficulties of Malory's spelling and use of archaic words. If I can do this and keep the wonder and the magic, I shall be pleased and gratified.

This rationale echoes his purpose for writing *East of Eden*: to leave a family history for his sons.

Perhaps most importantly, Steinbeck's study of Malory instilled in him the values of Arthur and his knights: "I think any sense of right and wrong, my feeling of nobless oblige, and any thought I may have against the oppressor and for the oppressed, came from this ... book." If true, Malory's influence must have been incalculable: siding with the oppressed, against the oppressor, is the theme, and the heart, of much of Steinbeck's work.

PRELUDE TO THE GRAPES OF WRATH

Many of Steinbeck's works of the 1930s are often regarded simply as precursors to *The Grapes of Wrath*. Indeed, the ideas for this novel churned in his imagination—fermenting, stewing, brewing—and thus became more and more potent with each passing work. Eventually, of course, the ideas reached critical mass, but the road to this point of creation had been long and circuitous for Steinbeck, beginning with college.

Although he studied intermittently at Stanford, he never attained a degree; instead, he began his apprenticeship as a writer, crafting short stories. When not writing, he chose to work in places that would later inform his writing, as would his experiences, and interactions with other people, on the job. He worked as a rancher, a deck hand, a cotton picker, as well as in other labor-intensive, low-paying jobs. But why did he do this? What attracted him to poverty-stricken migrant workers in particular? James Gray speculates:

> He found these occupations congenial because they brought him into intimate association with the great company of workers among whom he chose as friends long before he used them as models for characters in stories. These were men whose courage he admired, whose rejection of cant and hypocrisy he applauded, and whose "high survival quotient" became for him the essential proof of a human being's success. (Gray, 51)

In this way, the people at the bottom of society's ladder became Steinbeck's heroes, in his perspective and in his work.

Steinbeck's writing apprenticeship continued with the writing and publication of *The Harvest Gypsies: On the Road to the Grapes of Wrath*. This book consisted of seven feature-length newspaper stories which appeared in *The San Francisco News* between 5–12 October 1936. (They were also collected and printed as the pamphlet, called *Their Blood Is Strong*.) When Steinbeck wrote these dispatches in 1936, *Tortilla Flat* had already made him something of a celebrity, and *In Dubious Battle* had already established him as an authority on farm labor issues, particularly those dealing with displaced mid-westerners now toiling as California migrant workers (Wollenberg, vi). The proliferation of this ragged community in California prompted the editor for *The San Francisco News* to invite Steinbeck to write the series. And so, outfitting an old bread truck for the journey—similar to the way Steinbeck outfitted "Rocinante" for touring the U.S. with Charley several decades later—he spent much of the summer of 1936 traveling the state's agricultural centers, hoping to expose the laborers' appalling working and living conditions (vi–vii). But these seven articles not only represented the fruit of his firsthand observations; they also featured the kind of detached, factual reporting style that would reappear in the "interchapters" of *The Grapes of Wrath*, and still later in *East of Eden*.

Staggering details emerged from Steinbeck's reporting: for example, between 1935–1938, approximately 300,000 to 500,000 Okies—displaced Oklahomans—arrived in California (Wollenberg, xi), and at any one time, at least 150,000 homeless migrants scoured California seeking any form of employment, no matter how humiliating the work, no matter how low the wages, simply to stave off starvation for a few days more (19). In this context, Steinbeck began, but never finished, a novel entitled *The Oklahomans* (Demott, xxxiii), but *In Dubious Battle* continued the theme, showing what happens when migrant workers, goaded by two socialists, coalesce and strike. These literary rumblings and tremors portended the earthquake that would be *The Grapes of Wrath*.

In the meantime, however, *Of Mice and Men* escalated the country's sense of crisis. It displayed the loneliness and hopelessness of two migrant ranch-hands, George and Lennie, who dream of owning their own farm, clutching that dream like a security blanket, intuiting—but trying not to admit to themselves—that they will actually never realize their dream. Here, we see the personal side of migrants; they were, of course, ordinary people with dreams, limits, and, perhaps most importantly, feelings, including a searing, deep-seated sense of loneliness. George ruminates on the two men's isolation and its remedy, togetherness:

> George said, "Guys like us got no fambly. They make a little stake an' then they blow it in. They ain't got nobody in the worl' that gives a hoot in hell about 'em—"
> "But not us," Lennie cried happily. "Tell about us now."
> George was quiet for a moment. "But not us," he said. "Because—" "Because I got you an'—"
> "An I got you. We got each other, that's what, that gives a hoot in hell about us," Lennie cried in triumph.

The Grapes of Wrath enlarged upon this theme of loneliness and togetherness; *Of Mice and Men* was only the beginning.

The living and working conditions of migrant workers so infuriated Steinbeck that he wrote a book which bitterly criticized them: *L'Affaire Lettuceberg*. For some reason, though, Steinbeck felt it most prudent to burn the work. But the novel which followed, *The Grapes of Wrath*, rose from the ashes. It not only earned Steinbeck the Pulitzer Prize in 1940, it contributed to his winning The Nobel Peace Prize for Literature in 1962. At that time, he was only the sixth American author to win this most prestigious of prizes. More recently, in 1999, the editors of The Modern Library ranked *The Grapes of Wrath* the tenth best English-language novel, out of one hundred, from the last century; as an American novel, it was surpassed only by three other American works: *The Great Gatsby* (#2), *The Sound and the Fury* (#6), and *Catch 22* (#7).

Since it was first published, *The Grapes of Wrath* has sold more than 14 million copies, continues to sell approximately 100,000 paperback copies a year, and, according to Robert Demott, it has been translated into "nearly every language on earth" (Demott, xxii). The story relates the saga of the Joad family, a band of thirteen refugees fleeing the Oklahoma dust bowl. Originally, the group consisted of three generations: Grandma and Grandpa (both of whom die on the journey to California); their children: Pa Joad, Tom Joad (Pa's brother), and Ma Joad; and their children: Tom, the eldest, who, as the story begins, has just been freed from prison for manslaughter; Rose of Sharon, who is pregnant, and her husband, Connie Rivers, who later abandons her; Noah Joad, who is mentally retarded and who also abandons the family; Al Joad, who is good at tinkering with the engines of cars and the hearts of women; and two young children, Ruthie and Winfield. A non-family member comes along, too, however; Jim Casy, a former Christian minister seeking—and, at times, proclaiming—a new religion, a religion which has much in common with American Transcendentalism.

The Joads were traveling to California because several years of dust bowl conditions bankrupted them, and then they (and hundreds of thousands of other "Okies") were lured to California by promises of prosperity, promises that portrayed California as a land of milk and honey, where all would have jobs, and where each family could resume their life on their own piece of property. It is only later, when the Okies arrive in California, however, that they learn the bitter truth: the landowner associations deliberately overadvertised and overstated the number of jobs available to entice as many migrant laborers as possible.

Thus, with a surplus of labor, the landowners got away with paying bare-subsistence-level wages to increase their own profit margin.

The omniscient narrator explains an even more heinous atrocity:

> There is a crime here that goes beyond denunciation. There is a sorrow here that weeping cannot symbolize. There is a failure here that topples all our success. The fertile earth, the straight tree rows, the sturdy trunks, and the ripe fruit. And children dying of pellagra must die because a profit cannot be taken from an orange. And coroners must fill in the certificate—died of malnutrition—because the food must rot, must be forced to rot.
>
> The people come with nets to fish for potatoes in the river, and the guards hold them back; they come in rattling cars to get the dumped oranges, but the kerosene is sprayed. And they stand still and watch the potatoes float by, listen to the screaming pigs being killed in a ditch and covered with quick-lime, watch the mountains of oranges slop down to a putrefying ooze; in the eyes of the hungry there is a growing wrath. In the souls of the people the grapes of wrath are filling and growing heavy, growing heavy for the vintage.

This passage exemplifies not only the landowners' cruelty and greediness, but showcases a narrative device Steinbeck, ever the innovator, invented for *The Grapes of Wrath*, and later revisited in *East of Eden*. This quotation was culled from what is called an "interchapter," or "intercalary" chapter—material voiced by an impersonal, detached, third-person omniscient narrator.

Typically, Steinbeck alternates these "interchapters" with more conventional chapters: in *The Grapes of Wrath*, he wrote one about the Joads, then one about the plight of migrant workers more generally, providing the big picture as context. And as the subject matter shifts, so does the voice. In a typical interchapter, an omniscient narrator pans across a broad scene, which tends to make the Joads seem small, insignificant, even valueless; after all, the Joads just happen to be one family, among many desperate Okies, which the camera eye glimpses. But rather than pause to focus upon the Joads and evoke pity for their plight, the camera eye continues to arc across the scene, seemingly indifferent to the Joads', or anyone else's, suffering. (Indeed, this self-conscious display of indifference is reminiscent of nature's indifference in Stephen Crane's "The Open Boat," though the question of whether Steinbeck was a Naturalist is still debated.)[3] The interchapters, then, primarily serve to provide a larger context within which to better appreciate the Joads' saga.

In addition, the interchapters add texture and tone. One interchapter, for example, records the staccato, command-barking voice of a used car salesman as he unscrupulously herds helpless Okies across a dusty car lot to buy a rickety jalopy, which, he assures them, will carry them across the desert to California. From this perspective, readers get an overwhelming sense of the salesman's contempt: "There's a dumb-bunny lookin' at the Chrysler. Find out if he got any jack in his jeans. Some a these farm boys is sneaky. Soften 'em up an' roll 'em in to me, Joe [his partner]. You're doin' good." This same salesman later harangues a man who bought a car and wants his money back:

> Sure, we sold it. Guarantee? We guaranteed it to be an automobile. We didn't guarantee to wet-nurse it. Now listen here, you—you bought a car, an' now you're squawkin'. I don't give a damn if you don't make payments. We ain't got your paper. We turn that over to the finance company. They'll get after you, not us. We don't hold no paper. Yeah? Well you jus' get tough an' I'll call a cop. No, we did not switch the tires. Run 'im outa here, Joe. He bought a car, an' now he ain't satisfied.

Thus, when Steinbeck juxtaposes the car salesman's harsh, indifferent voice with the voices of the spirit-broken Okie families, he is able to highlight more dramatically the sellers' cruelty and bravado. Furthermore, this effect also resonates in chapter three, a vitally important interchapter that focuses on a turtle's relentless trek southwestward. No matter if someone kicks the turtle, or a car swerves to hit it, it rights itself and continues on its journey. The turtle displays the same tenacity and resilience that the Joad family displays when they, too, must overcome obstacles, traveling toward California.

Although Steinbeck immerses the reader in the Okies' suffering, the Joad family's positive transformation emerges from it, and the novel thus provides hope. At first, the Joads practice, and act upon, an every-family-for-itself philosophy, but as they suffer, and as they observe the suffering of other migrants, the Joads soften and come to identify with their fellows, broadening their definition of "family." To the Joads, "family" no longer signifies just blood relatives; rather, it's newly defined as anyone in need. As Ma Joad memorably states, "Use' ta be the fambly was fust. It ain't so now. It's anybody. Worse off we get, the more we got to do." This transformation is registered, in one way, by the way the Joads' come to use the words "I" and "we." As "we" expands and expands to encompass all people, it teaches the Joads two truths: the entire human race is a family, and people are responsible for everyone in their extended family, not just their blood relatives.

The Joads learn and relearn this lesson every evening when they pitch camp in a ditch with twenty other families, as described by the omniscient narrator of an interchapter: "In the evening a strange thing happened: the twenty families became one family, the children were the children of all ... In the evening, sitting about the fires, the twenty were one." Similarly, the novel's readers eavesdrop as the men gather that night to talk:

> D'ja hear about the kid in the fourth tent down?
> No, I jus' come in.
> Well, that kid's been a-crying in his sleep an'a rollin in his sleep. Them folks thought he got worms. So they give him a blaster, an' he died. It was what they call black-tongue the kid had. Comes from not getting' good things to eat.
> Poor little fella.
> Yeah, but them folks can't bury him. Got to go to the county stone orchard.
> Well, hell.
> And hands went into pockets and little coins came out. In front of the tent a little heap of silver grew. And the family found it there.

One of Steinbeck's greatest achievements, as displayed here, was his ability to capture and recreate the idiom of migrant workers. Certainly, this was one of many reasons for the novel's recognition—via prizes, awards, and sales—as one of America's greatest novels.

The works Steinbeck produced in the 1940s and early 1950s, however, elicited mixed reactions; often, the books pleased the public, but disappointed critics, who felt that Steinbeck failed to sustain the same level of artistry demonstrated in *The Grapes of Wrath*. While that may be true, and while Steinbeck's works varied in quality, these works should not be dismissed. True, during this period, Steinbeck wrote shorter books on less serious, often allegorical, topics—including *Cannery Row*, *The Pearl*, and *The Wayward Bus*—but does that make them failures? Indeed, *The Wayward Bus*, like *The Canterbury Tales*, explored the unpredictable ways people behave when crowded together; or, to look at it another way, since the bus carries characters from all walks of life, the bus could be viewed as a microcosm of society, with characters interacting with much the same humor, animation, and animosity as Chaucer's. Also, Steinbeck expanded his repertoire during this time to include the stage and screen work, involved in twelve screenplays between 1940 and 1957. In short, disregarding Steinbeck's work from this era would prevent readers from fully comprehending the scope of his literary achievement.

For example, *Cannery Row*, a sequel to *Tortilla Flat*, features a comic exterior, including a hysterical frog hunt scene, but readers soon discover a devastatingly satirical novel—"a poisonous cream puff," as Steinbeck described it. Instead of paisanos, it features Anglos as wino-bums, sleeping in the shacks and water pipes of vacant lots in Monterey. Mack, their leader, resembles Danny, just as "the boys" recall Danny's cohorts. And while it is true that they fight, drink, steal, and avoid work and responsibility as much as possible, how bad can this lifestyle be when contrasted with that of the average middle-class white capitalist? Here, Steinbeck juxtaposes the two lifestyles:

> [Mack and the boys] ... are the Virtues, the Graces, the Beauties of the mangled craziness of Monterey and the cosmic Monterey where men in fear and hunger destroy their stomachs in the fight to secure certain food, where men hungering for love destroy everything lovable about them. Mack and the boys are the Beauties, the Virtues, the Graces. In the world ruled by tigers with ulcers, rutted by strictured bulls, scavenged by blind jackals, Mack and the boys dine delicately with the tigers, fondle the frantic heifers, and wrap

up the crumbs to feed the sea gulls of Cannery Row. What can it profit a man to gain the whole world and to come to his property with a gastric ulcer, a blown prostrate, and bifocals? Mack and the boys avoid that trap, walk around the poison, step over the noose while a generation of trapped, poisoned, and trussed-up men scream at them and call them no-goods, come-to-bad-ends, blots-on-the-town, thieves, rascals, bums. Our father who art in nature ... must have a great and overwhelming love for no-goods and blots-on-the-town and bums, and Mack and the boys. Virtues and graces and laziness and zest. Our Father who art in nature.

Like the men with whom Steinbeck worked while in and out of college, Mack and the boys have a "high survival quotient."

But unlike the political satire underlying *Cannery Row, A Russian Journal*—one of Steinbeck's four travelogues and a grossly under appreciated part of his corpus—possessed a graver atmosphere, published, as it was, in the nascent stages of the Cold War. The book's inception, as an idea, came in 1946 when Steinbeck and renowned photographer Robert Capa sat commiserating about life at the bar of New York City's Bedford Hotel. There, they discussed the news coverage of Russia in particular; the U.S. media, made anxious by the growing tension of the Cold War, presented Russians at this time as one-dimensional characters: that is, the enemy. Steinbeck and Capa—cajoled by Willy the bartender, whose kibitzing and drink-pouring made the whole scheme seem all the more plausible—intuited that there had to be more to the Russians than met the eye; in fact, they sensed that "there were some things that nobody wrote about Russia, and these were the things that interested [Steinbeck and Capa] most of all." What were those things? Just the simple details of everyday life in Russia: "What do the people wear there? What do they serve at dinner? How do they make love, and how do they die? What do they talk about?" In other words, as these two men attempted to imagine what life was like in Russia, they became convinced that "there must be a private life of the Russian people," and that the only reason Americans did not know about it was that no one had yet written about, or photographed, it. And that's where they came in.

Their casual conversations, then, evolved into a project with strictly outlined goals: "we would try to do honest reporting, to set down what we saw and heard without editorial comment, without drawing conclusions about things we didn't know sufficiently." And above all else, they vowed to "avoid all politics," as Steinbeck noted: "All we wanted to do was to report what Russian people were like." To this end, from July 31st to approximately mid-September 1946, Steinbeck and Capa exhausted themselves crossing Russia. Their polite Russian hosts guided their visits to practically every cultural monument or event imaginable: Lenin's tomb; a circus; a museum in Georgia that commemorated Stalin's early life; puppet shows; dramatic presentations, both small and large venues; a factory where tractors were built; formal dinners; dance-parties at nightclubs; an air show; parks; the ballet; small-town farming communities; and much more. Capa, for his part, took 4,000 negatives in 40 days, and ultimately, the work of the two men showed Americans that they were not so different from ordinary Russians, a gesture meant to unify rather than divide these two world powers at such a crucial juncture in history.

Politics aside, however, the more fascinating subject of *A Russian Journal* is the nature of the relationship between Steinbeck and Capa, reported through the prism of Steinbeck's witty, wry perspective—a caustic voice similar to the one Steinbeck later adopted again for *Travels With Charley*. As our tourguide, Steinbeck makes even the most mundane things humorous, particularly when contrasted against the drab, dreary, gray setting of Russia. Consider, for example, the two men's arrival in Moscow. After a long, grueling trip—at times aboard a C-47 American cargo plane—Steinbeck and Capa arrive to find that their contact man, Joe Newman, is out of town, leaving Steinbeck and Capa exhausted, bewildered, and lost in a strange city. Though some fellow Americans rescued them, and pumped them full of smoked salmon and vodka, the two men still (understandably) harbored a grudge against the hapless Newman:

> After a while we didn't feel lonely and lost any more. We decided to move into Joe Newman's room to punish him. We used his towels, and his soap, and his toilet paper. We drank his whisky. We slept on his couch and his bed. We thought that was the least he could do for us, to repay us for having been miserable. The fact that he didn't know that we were coming, we argued, was no excuse for him, and he had to be

punished. And so we drank his two bottles of Scotch whisky. It must be admitted that we didn't know at that time what a crime this was. There is considerable dishonesty and chicanery among American newspapermen in Moscow, but it has never reached the level to which we brought it.

As anyone knows—especially those who have read *The Canterbury Tales* or even Steinbeck's own *The Wayward Bus*—over the course of a long journey, people's nerves are bound to fray, and personality clashes escalate to explosions. Indeed, the interpersonal relations among the people who appear in *A Russian Journal* form a story within the story, and these often entertain readers more than the ostensible subject. In part, this stems from Steinbeck's ability to almost always find a humorous way to explain why he and Capa are getting on each other's nerves. For example, Steinbeck volunteers a critique of "an unpleasant quality in Capa's nature": "He is a bathroom hog." Steinbeck here ostensibly warns any woman who temporarily loses her sanity and actually considers marrying Capa, and to reinforce the point, Steinbeck later indicts Capa of a crime of much greater magnitude: he steals others' books. Steinbeck puts this crime in context for the potential, future Mrs. Capa:

> Among Moscow correspondents, particularly in the winter, a code of honor has grown up, rather like the code which developed in the West concerning horses, and it is nearly a matter for lynching to steal a man's book. But Capa never learned and never reformed. Right to the end of his Russian stay he stole books. He also steals women and cigarettes, but this can be more easily forgiven.

But even though this was Steinbeck's book, he allowed Capa to interpose, between chapters six and seven—seemingly a propos of nothing—a critique against Steinbeck entitled "A Legitimate Complaint." It begins with words reminiscent of those uttered at the beginning of Dostoevsky's Notes from the Underground: "I am not happy at all." What follows, of course, are three and a half pages of grousing about the trip in general, and about Steinbeck in particular. For example, Capa recounts the way Steinbeck arranged for them to tour the Soviet Union:

> First he told the Russians that it was a mistake to regard him as the pillar of the world proletariat, indeed he could rather be described as a representative of Western decadence, indeed as far west as the lowest dives in California. Also he committed himself to write only the truth, and when he was asked politely what truth was, he answered, "This I do not know." After this promising beginning, he jumped out of a window and broke his knee.

If writing is to delight and as well as instruct, then such good-natured raillery pair up well with the factual elements of *A Russian Journal.*

One of Steinbeck's least successful works, *Burning Bright* (subtitled "A Play in Story Form,") was the third, last, and worst of Steinbeck's experiments in the play-novelette, a form he created and used earlier for *Of Mice and Men* and *The Moon is Down.* The title, *Burning Bright,* originates from William Blake's poem, "The Tyger," which also serves as the book's epigraph:

> Tyger! Tyger! Burning bright
> In the forests of the night,
> What immortal hand or eye
> Could frame thy fearful symmetry?

The story unfolds over the course of three acts, with each set in a different location: Act I, at the circus, where the protoganists work; Act II, at the farm, where they now work. And Act III has two scenes: one aboard the ship, where they now work, and one in the hospital, where the female protagonist, Mordeen, has just had her baby.

Mordeen, wife of John Saul (the protagonist), loves her husband so much that she would do anything for him, thus leading to the play's conflict: Joe Saul, a man approaching middle age, is impotent, but doesn't know it. For all his married life, he has craved fatherhood, and simultaneously, one of Joe Saul's subordinates, Mr. Victor, lusts for Mordeen, pining for the chance to have sex with her. Thus, Mordeen faces a dilemma: does she decline Victor's offer and thereby ensure that Joe Saul will never have the children he so desperately wants; or does she have sex with Victor to bring Joe Saul a baby—albeit a child not his own? Mordeen labors over this decision, its weight compounded by

Victor's incessant nagging, until finally she succumbs. The story's climax occurs when Joe realizes that he is not the father but, despite his hurt feelings, defies his every instinct and chooses to accept the child as his own.

Just as the Joads spiritually grow when they expand their definition of family to include everyone, so Joe Saul emotionally evolves when he transitions from believing that the child is simply his child, to considering any child to be as important as his own:

> [Formerly,] I thought, I felt, I knew that that particular seed [i.e., his own] has importance over other seed. I thought that was what I had to give. It is not so. I know it now ... It is the race, the species that must go staggering on. Mordeen, our ugly little species, weak and ugly, torn with insanities, violent and quarrelsome, sensing evil—the only species that knows evil and practices it—the only one that senses cleanness and is dirty, that knows about cruelty and is unbearably cruel ... The baby is alive ... The spark continues—a new human—[the] only being of its kind anywhere—that has struggled without strength when every force of tooth and claw, of storm and cloud, of lightning and germs was against it—struggled and survived, survived even the self-murdering instinct.

Steinbeck revisits the epigraph from Blake as he ponders the newborn: "what animal has made beauty, created it, save only we? With all our horrors and our faults, somewhere in us there is a shining. That is the most important of all facts. There is a shining." To reach this epiphany, Joe Saul, like his predecessor Jim Casy from *The Grapes of Wrath*, had to undergo a grueling transformation process: "I had to walk into the black to know—to know that every man is father to all children and every child must have all men as father. This is not a little piece of private property, registered and fenced and separated. Mordeen! This is the Child." To further signify Joe Saul's transformation, Steinbeck directs Saul to tear the operating room mask from his face, to reveal how "his face was shining and his eyes were shining." Like his namesake, Saul has had the scales removed from his eyes and now sees life in a new light.

Next, the book *Once There Was a War* anthologized sixty-one articles Steinbeck wrote for the *New York Herald-Tribune* Syndicate during World War II. But why is Steinbeck, in 1958, resurrecting war correspondence from fifteen years before?

> For what they are worth, or for what they may recapture, here they are, period pieces, fairy tales, half-meaningless memories of a time and of attitudes which have gone forever from the world, a sad and jocular recording of a little part of a war I saw and do not believe, unreal with trumpted-up pageantry ... The pieces in this volume were written under pressure and in tension ... Their very raggedness, it seems to me, a parcel of their immediacy. They are as real as the wicked witch and the good fairy, as true and tested and edited as a war myth.

These collected dispatches span 20 June 1943 to 13 December 1943; came from Italy, England, and North Africa; and each was approximately 1,000 words long. The topics cover a wide range: the actual war, such as what men experienced when they travel by troopship or practiced assaulting beach fortifications; many sketches depicted the sights, sounds, and people of these foreign locales for curious readers back home, such as the way the English, for their American guests' benefit, celebrate July 4th, or the way the people of Dover tenaciously tend their gardens, despite frequent bombardment. And although covering a war obliged Steinbeck, at times, to focus mostly upon war's grim realities—the loneliness, carnage, and destruction that make war hell—he nevertheless seized every opportunity to inject levity into situations that so desperately needed it, much as he did in *A Russian Journal*. For example, several dispatches charted the antics of a loveable goldbricker named Private "Big Train" Mulligan, and another dispatch was devoted to detailing the idiosyncrasies of an alcoholic goat, the mascot of a British airport's personnel.

But all these lesser-known works aside, this era of Steinbeck's career is most noteworthy for its production of the two works that were considered by many to be Steinbeck's lesser masterpieces: *East of Eden*, and *The Sea of Cortez*.

EAST OF EDEN

Many believe that *East of Eden* is Steinbeck's second-most important novel, surpassed only by *The Grapes of Wrath*; indeed, Steinbeck himself considered *Eden* to be his magnum opus, the crowning achievement of his life's work. Similar to how Steinbeck spent years researching and reflecting on Zapata, and similar to how Steinbeck gradually put the pieces together for *The Grapes of Wrath* in the 1930's, the writer let *East of Eden* gestate in his mind for decades. He thus "nurtured" it "all of his life and ... [it] seemed to grow with him until the time of writing was at hand" (Timmerman, 210). Readers find evidence of this in Steinbeck's letters, which pinpoint specific points in the novel's growth. For example, to one correspondent, Steinbeck placed *East of Eden* in the context of his life and work, concluding, "That earlier work was practice for this ... The rest was practice" (211). In another letter, Steinbeck asserted, "I still think it is The Book, as far as I am concerned. Always before I have held something back for later. Nothing is held back here. This is not practice for a future. This is what I have practiced for" (212). However, in spite of Steinbeck's years of planning, critics and scholars generally didn't find the novel as satisfying as *The Grapes of Wrath*.

Critic Warren French observed, "For John Steinbeck, *East of Eden* was the consummation of the efforts to find a hero among the folk—a magnificent effort at a second epic to match *The Grapes of Wrath*," but French believed Steinbeck ultimately failed to reach this goal. Timmerman, meanwhile, argued that *East of Eden* explored themes Steinbeck had pondered for his entire life: "*East of Eden* was to be the focal point for the moral views about humankind and human relationships that he had been developing since the early thirties" (Timmerman, 212). To do this, Steinbeck looked back to, and used, stories from his own family mythology.

Originally entitled *Salinas Valley, East of Eden* was intended to chronicle the history of Steinbeck's mother's side of the family (the Hamiltons). However, as Steinbeck labored at crafting the novel, two related plots gradually emerged: one concerning the Trask family—particularly Adam Trask—and one concerning Cathy Ames, a woman who was temporarily his wife. To chronicle the family saga, Steinbeck revisited the narrative technique he had used so successfully in *The Grapes of Wrath*: the intercalary/interchapter. Lester Jay Marks argues that Steinbeck used the Hamilton sections much as he used the interchapters in *The Grapes of Wrath:* "to reflect and generalize action that has occurred, or to signal action that is to come ... and to serve ... as a broad backdrop on which to paint the geographical, social, and cultural conditions of the Salinas Valley and nineteenth century California" (Marks, 117, 118). Timmerman concurs:

> it is clear that [Steinbeck] saw modern civilization as threatening the spirit of man and the individual creative consciousness. The intercalary chapters of the novel evoke that threat as surely as they did in *The Grapes of Wrath*, with the exception that here [*East of Eden*] they are general and wide-ranging, like a vast curtain of events against which the Trasks and Hamiltons work out their particular story, while in *The Grapes of Wrath* the intercalary chapters always focus sharply and urgently on the narration and the immediacy of the Okie migration. That external world of *East of Eden* is vast and fairly amorphous in its generalized threat, yet parallels the narrower struggle captured in the narrative. (Timmerman, 228)

Style notwithstanding, however, Steinbeck had primarily intended to record this family history for his sons' benefit, so they would know who they were and where they had come from. He also wanted, through the novel, to teach his sons "one of the greatest, perhaps the greatest story of all—the story of good and evil, of strength and weakness, of love and hate, of beauty and goodness" (Timmerman, 218).

Regarding the novel's structure, Steinbeck divided the novel into four parts: Part I spans the years 1862–1900, telling the story of Adam Trask's birth, and the sibling rivalry that emerges between him and his half-brother Charles, as the two boys grew to become men; for years, Adam served in the army and wandered the country, while Charles stayed at the farm and cultivated it. Part II covers the years 1900–1902—the period in which Adam brings his bride, Cathy Ames, from Connecticut to the Salinas Valley. Though she tries to abort the babies in her womb, she fails and gives birth to twin boys: Aron and Caleb. Not only does Cathy bite the hand of Samuel Hamilton, the man who delivered the babies, but almost immediately after their birth, she shoots

Adam, abandons the family, and becomes a prostitute in a local whorehouse. These events so dispirit Adam that for 11 years, he does not even bother to name his children, much less raise them, nor does he till his fertile land. As a result, most of the fatherly duties fall on the shoulders of a house-servant, a wise Chinese man named Lee.

Part III, which covers the years 1911–1912, is devoted to the Hamilton family—all of Samuel's children and their accomplishments, including how Samuel revived Adam from his paralyzing melancholy. In Part IV, which spans 1912–1918, Adam takes Aron and Caleb, his twin sons, to live in Salinas, and the novel ends with Adam's death. Attentive readers of the novel will notice recurring symbols, as well as a pattern: first, east of Eden is the region where Adam and Eve settled after their expulsion from Paradise, and thus, presumably, it is the setting for the Cain-Abel story. And, speaking of the biblical story of Cain and Abel, all of the major characters in *East of Eden* have names that begin with a "C" (Charles, Caleb) or an "A" (Adam, Aron); the "C" characters represent Cain's legacy, while the "A" characters represent Abel's, and each generation re-enacts, in its own way, the Cain-Abel story, which serves as the novel's thematic core.

Lee stated that the Cain-Abel story "is the best-known story in the world because it is everybody's story ... this old and terrible story is important because it is a chart of the soul—the secret, rejected, guilty soul." The particular language and content of the story, found in the book of Genesis (4:1-11), greatly informs a more comprehensive reading of Steinbeck's novel:

> Now Adam knew Eve, his wife, and she conceived and bore Cain, and said, "I have gotten a man from the Lord."
>
> Then she bore again, this time his brother Abel. Now Abel was a keeper of sheep, but Cain was a tiller of the ground.
>
> And in the process of time it came to pass that Cain brought an offering of the fruit of the ground to the Lord.
>
> Abel also brought of the firstlings of his flock and of their fat. And the Lord respected Abel and his offering,
>
> But he did not respect Cain and his offering. And Cain was very angry, and his countenance fell.
>
> So the Lord said to Cain, "Why are you angry? And why has your countenance fallen?"

If you do well, will you not be accepted? And if you do not do well, sin lies at the door. And its desire is for you, but you shall rule over it.

Now Cain talked with Abel his brother; and it came to pass, when they were in the field, that Cain rose against Abel his brother and killed him.

Then the Lord said to Cain, "Where is Abel your brother?" And he said, "I do not know. Am I my brother's keeper?"

And he [the Lord] said, "What have you done? The voice of your brother's blood cries out to me from the ground."

"So now you are cursed from the earth, which has opened its mouth to receive your brother's blood from your hand." (Gen 4:1-11, emphasis added to verse 7).

In part one of Steinbeck's novel, both Charles and Adam present birthday gifts to their father, Cyrus Trask; Adam's gift is a mongrel pup, while Charles' gift is a pocket knife—a knife so expensive that Charles had to work extra hard to purchase it. Charles desperately wants to please his father, yet for no discernable reason, Cyrus joyfully accepts Adam's gift (the pup) but receives Charles' gift (the pocketknife) with no apparent appreciation, much less enthusiasm. Charles feels slighted and stings from his father's rejection, and like Cain, Charles soon sets out to punish Adam. First, Charles beats Adam, and then, while Charles rushes home to retrieve a hatchet with which to kill Adam, Adam manages to roll over into a ditch. Charles returns with the hatchet and the intent to murder Adam, but due to the night's darkness, he cannot discern Adam lying breathless in the ditch. Charles hurls the hatchet into the fields and proceeds to go to town to get drunk, and though things eventually blow over, Adam's and Charles' relationship is never the same.

The Cain-Abel story is again re-enacted in the second generation of the Trask family. While living in Salinas, Adam conceives of a risky but potentially profitable scheme, inventing a method for packing California lettuce in ice so that when it arrived in New York, it would be fresh and edible. He perfectly packs the lettuce, and as the whole town cheers, the train sets out for New York. Unfortunately, though, due to mishaps completely out of his control, the train ride takes too long, and consequently the heat not only melts the ice, but also putrifies the lettuce. Thus, the entire venture became a disaster. Caleb sees his father's pain regarding this disappointment and desperately wants to please him, so he decides that he will, through his own labors, recoup the money and present it to Adam as a present. To this end, Caleb works hard, raising a crop of beans, and reaps a big profit. However, when he presents the profit—his gift—to Adam, Adam rejects it. Adam, instead, informs Caleb that he wishes Caleb were more like Aron, a student at Stanford (where Steinbeck himself had studied). Once again, the father's rejection hurts Caleb so deeply that he decides to punish Aron by taking him to their mother's whorehouse, the mother Aron had always believed was dead.

Learning the truth about his mother so disillusions and hurts Aron that he joins the army and, while serving his tour of duty during World War I, he is killed in action. Caleb, stung with remorse, believes it is his fault when Aron dies, since he took Aron to meet their mother, but the novel ends with Adam on his deathbed, releasing Caleb from all guilt. The word Adam speaks to absolve Caleb—"timshel"—is probably the most important word in the novel, resonating, and encapsulating, the novel's main themes. The word originates from the Cain-Abel story, wherein God informs Cain that he still has the capability of presenting an offering that will please him: "If you do well, will you not be accepted?" Thus, Cain still has the ability and freewill to do good, though he also has the ability and freewill to do evil, as noted in verse seven: "And if you do not do well, sin lies at the door. And its desire is for you, but you shall rule over it."

The key phrase here comes at the end: "but you shall rule over it." Adam Trask, his servant Lee, and other biblical scholars spend years trying to determine the exact meaning of this Hebrew phrase. Does "you shall" mean that Cain was predestined to resist this particular temptation? The answer is unclear, but eventually, they all arrive at what they believe to be the correct interpretation: the words "but you shall rule over it" come from the Hebrew word "Timshel," which means, roughly, "you have the freewill to do good or evil." Thus, the freewill God has given man is the greatest gift God could give, as Milton also argues in *Paradise Lost*. It confers dignity upon man and gives man hope. With this in mind, Steinbeck appears to go to great lengths to stress that the mark upon Cain was not meant to oppress him, but to do exactly the opposite: to warn people against harming him. This divine warning to others protects Cain and thereby gives him hope.

Critics generally agree that the Cain-Abel story thematically applies not merely to the novel's characters, but to all humankind. Howard Levant observed, "The timshel doctrine enables Steinbeck to broaden an autobiographical novel into the spiritual autobiography of mankind, of life itself" (Timmerman, 216). Ultimately, of course, the "timshel" doctrine and the Cain-Abel struggle hint at the most fundamental conflict in human history: the struggle between good and evil, as Steinbeck himself explained:

> I believe that there is one story in the world, and only one, that has frightened and inspired us ... Humans are caught— in their lives, in their thoughts, in their hungers and ambitions, in their avarice and cruelty, and in their kindness and generosity too—in a net of good and evil. I think this is the only story we have and ... it occurs on all levels of feeling and intelligence ... All novels, all poetry, are built on the never-ending contest in ourselves of good and evil.

Like Cain, we, too, continually experience, within ourselves, the struggle between good or evil, and *East of Eden* explores this struggle in multiple ways. The character of Cathy Ames, for example, represents the embodiment of irredeemable evil. According to Timmerman,

> The heart of *East of Eden*, and it is a black and perverse heart, is Cathy Ames. She represents a dark force unleashed in the world, a dark principle in relation to which other characters must order their lives ... each [character] attains thematic clarity when understood in relation to her. She is the pivot for Steinbeck's moral vision; the actions of the characters in relation to her represent his answers to her and the articulation of his moral vision. (Timmerman, 247)

Conversely, Samuel Hamilton represents the other side of the spectrum—man's potential for good: "Samuel is the measure of man's spirit to endure and to work a good work" (Timmerman 24). Everything thus hinges, ultimately, upon the "timshel" doctrine, which suggests that all people can have hope because God has endowed humans with the ability, and freewill, to choose, though with this ability, of course, comes great responsibility.

In addition to *East of Eden*, the gem of this epoch in Steinbeck's career is *Sea of Cortez: A Leisurely Journal of Travel and Research*.[4] In this book, Steinbeck recounts the 1940 sea voyage down the California and Mexican coastline, and back, to discover and catalogue marine life. And because Ed Ricketts, the leader of the expedition, was later killed in 1948 in a car accident, Steinbeck wrote and inserted a biographical segment entitled "About Ed Ricketts" in the 1951 version. As a marine biologist and philosopher, Ricketts became the template for Steinbeck's philosopher heroes, such as Lee in *East of Eden*, though a more obvious example is the character "Doc," an actual marine biologist, who appears in *Cannery Row*, *Sweet Thursday*, and Steinbeck's short story, "The Snake" from *The Long Valley*.

But in *Sea of Cortez*, Steinbeck's diary entries often become lengthy philosophical meditations, occasioned by his observations about marine life; Steinbeck came to believe that human life was much like marine life, and, therefore, studying marine life enhanced one's understanding of human life, and vice versa. A recurring image demonstrates this correlation: the image of the marine biologist studying the tidal pools which remain after the tide has receded. All the marine life in the tidal pool makes it a microcosm for the macrocosm, the ocean, just as a group of humans—such as the bus passengers in *The Wayward Bus*—is a microcosm for the macrocosm, that is, humanity.

Reportedly, Steinbeck had a "lifelong passion" (Astro, 65) for trying to understand the relationship between the individual and the group. In fact, sometime between 1934–1936, Steinbeck wrote a paper about group behavior entitled "Argument of Phalanx" ("phalanx" refers to the battle formation assumed by of a company of individual Roman foot-soldiers); ultimately, after Steinbeck studied the behavior of both animals (particularly fish) and humans, he came to believe that when individuals form a group, to an extent, they lose their individuality and replace it with a group identity. For example, when a single fish joins a school of fish, the school of fish acts as one, having a will and purpose of its own. The group thus becomes more than the sum of its parts, and the same observations apply to humans: "man is a double thing—a group animal and at the same time an individual" (Astro, 65). The result is what Steinbeck calls "group-man," and although this hypothesis has flaws, it provided Steinbeck with a theme that pervaded his work: "each character who forfeits his individuality violates his own integrity" (63). This idea also provides insight into the mob behavior displayed in, for example, *In Dubious Battle*.

However, the most important idea Steinbeck learned from Ricketts was so fundamental that it constituted a paradigm shift—that is, a wholly new perspective: "non-teleological" thinking, also known as "is thinking." Teleological thinking searches for causes and effects, for what could or should be, while non-teleological thinking focuses on what is (hence "is" or "as is" thinking). In other words, non-teleological thinking seeks to understand what something is—not why it is that way nor what it could or should be—because, logically, one must first understand the way things are before extrapolating inferences about the past or future. Indeed, the present is so rich and complex that it provides a person with more than enough to think about.

To put it another way: people often under-appreciate the present and then, on the basis of an uninformed view of the present, they try to build upon it premises leading to a conclusion, and thus, teleological thinkers may slight the present simply by way of denial; i.e., they refuse to face life as it actually is. Although this may be an oversimplification, the non-teleological thinker argues that things are the way they are because that is the way things are. According to Steinbeck, "The truest reason for anything's being so is that it is."

Later, when Steinbeck wrote *America and Americans*, his last book, he appears to have recaptured his sense of his country. Each of the work's nine chapters consists of two related parts: an essay and a montage of photographs, the two combining to convey each chapter's theme. Some themes are relatively benign—such as Americans' restlessness, attitudes towards the government, or feelings about the acquisition of wealth—but others address more volatile issues, such as racial tension. But no matter the theme, Steinbeck approaches it as a fiercely patriotic American. Each chapter, he declares,

> is informed by America and inspired by curiosity, impatience, some anger, and a passionate love of America and Americans. For I believe that out of the whole body of our past, out of our differences, our quarrels, our many interests and directions, something has emerged that is itself unique in the world: America—complicated, paradoxical, bullheaded, shy, cruel, boisterous, unspeakably dear, and very beautiful

Sentiments such as those expressed in *America and Americans* resurrect a question that begs to be settled: was Steinbeck a communist or a crypto-socialist?

Most likely, the answer is no, a conclusion based not only on the fierce patriotism that pervades his last book, but also by virtue of the way Steinbeck portrayed communists in his other works. Communists, as well as their ideological philosophies, are explored, evaluated, and rejected most explicitly in *In Dubious Battle*, a novel which, if anything, would provide Steinbeck with the most opportune time to advance socialism as an answer, if not *the* answer, to America's horrific labor problems in the 1930's, problems that were also explored in, for example, *The Harvest Gypsies*, *Of Mice and Men*, and *The Grapes of Wrath*.

In Dubious Battle begins almost in medias res. The greedy owners of apple orchards in the Torgas Valley have just lowered wages to bare-subsistence levels. Mack and Jim, two communist party workers, know that the owners' decision to slash wages will infuriate migrant workers, most of whom are dispossessed Midwesterners. They intend to seize this opportunity to foment the workers' anger and channel it into a strike, which they hope will lead to strikes in the cotton fields and elsewhere. Mac and Jim believe that, cumulatively, the strikes will undermine the capitalist system, or, even better, swell the communist party's ranks.

However, from the beginning, Steinbeck portrays Mac, the veteran party worker, and Jim, the novice, as unsympathetic characters. Not only do they lie, deceive, and demagogue; worst of all, they care nothing for the strikers they are ostensibly helping. For example, just as they arrive at the strikers' camp, a woman is howling in pain from the contractions that precede childbirth. To make matters worse, no one on hand seems to know how to deliver the baby, but Mac steps up, pretending to be experienced in such matters, and delivers the baby; afterwards, as he walks away, Mac admits to Jim that he had lied in order to seize the opportunity to ingratiate himself with the strikers, thus disregarding the health of the mother and child.

What brought Mac to such callousness? Years of party activity seem to have cauterized Mac's conscience, and at one point, he admonishes Jim, saying, "Don't you go liking people, Jim. We can't waste time liking people." Mac displays this same coldness when vigilantes burn the barn of Mr. Anderson, the landowner who was so courageous as to break ranks with the other landowners, and so kind as to allow the strikers to pitch camp on his land. In response to Doc Burton's expression of sympathy for Anderson, "Mac said harshly, 'We can't help it, Doc. He happens to be the one that's sacrificed for the men ... We can't think about the hurts of one man.'" Mac continues: "'I'm too busy with big bunches of men.'" As these passages demonstrate, Steinbeck appears to have ascertained, and openly critiqued, communism's problems regarding practical application, thus showing an American audience the incongruity of the political theory and its necessarily de-humanizing implementation.

Thus, Mac and Jim do not consider the strikers as fellow humans, but rather as materials to be used for political ends. When Jim asks Mac how they are to go about their work, Mac replies, "Well, there's just one rule—use whatever material you've got." Later, an elderly apple-picker named Dan falls from his ladder and dies, and Mac coldly calculates, "The old buzzard was worth something after all ... We can use him now," and Mac puts old Dan's body on display to enrage the strikers. Mac's, and Jim's, cold-bloodedness is underscored again when a striker, Joy, is shot dead by vigilante deputies, hired by the landowners association; referring to the Joy's corpse, which Mac later dismisses as "a lump of dirt," Mac urges the men, "We've got to use him to step our guys up, to keep 'em together. This'll stick 'em together, this'll make 'em fight." Mortified, one of the strikers "grimaced" and lectures Mac: "You're a cold-blooded bastard. Don't you think of nothing but 'strike'? ... [Joy was a] pal of yours, and you won't let him rest now. You want to use him. You're a pair of cold-blooded bastards." And Doc Burton seems to say it all when he shakes his head in disbelief and tells Mac, "you're the craziest mess of cruelty and haus-frau sentimentality, of clear vision and rose-colored glasses I ever saw. I don't know how you manage to be all of them at once."

Of course, it is primarily through Doc Burton that Steinbeck articulates his criticism of Mac, Jim, and their cause. When Mac criticizes Doc for having feelings—feelings that get in the way of business—Doc replies, "You practical men always lead practical men with stomachs. And something always gets out of hand. Your men get out of hand, they don't follow the rules of common sense, and you practical men either deny that it is so, or refuse to think about it. And when someone wonders what it is that makes a man with a stomach something more than your rule allows, why you howl, 'Dreamer, mystic, metaphysician.'" Mac retorts: "We've got a job to do ... we've got no time to mess around with high-falutin ideas." That, Doc replies, is precisely their problem: "Yes, and so you start your work not knowing your medium. And your ignorance trips you up every time." To put it in terms of *The Sea of Cortez*, Mac—and communists more generally—focus so much on the future, particularly the utopia socialism postulates, that they fail to appreciate the present. Not appreciating the present sufficiently constitutes the "ignorance [which] trips ... [them] up every time."

But the communists' problem is far graver than ignorance, willful blindness, or teleological thinking. Whereas Mac and Jim sacrifice people to the cause, Doc Burton devotes himself to people, not the cause. He explains to Mac, "I don't believe in the cause, but I believe in men." Mystified, unable to even conceive of such selflessness, Mac wonders, "What do you mean?" Doc replies, "I don't know. I guess I just believe they're men, and not animals ... I have some skill in helping men, and when I see some who need help, I just do it. I don't think about it much." Doc Burton's sentiments, combined with Steinbeck's condemnation of Mac and Jim, therefore appear to invalidate speculation concerning Steinbeck's sympathies toward communism.

But if Steinbeck did not embrace the tenets of socialism, then what beliefs did he embrace? Doc Burton, the character inspired by Ed Ricketts, both exemplifies and articulates many of them. Doc is a recurring character type, the hero character Lester Marks calls the "biological philosopher." Like Doc Burton, the philosopher-hero "looms outside and above the group[,] viewing the group with detached compassion." He is "an outsider who speculates on the group from the biologist's ... point of view." In one example, referring back to *In Dubious Battle*, Doc Burton tries to explain his point of view to Mac: "My senses aren't above reproach, but they're all I have. I want to see the whole picture—as nearly as I can. I don't want to put on the blinders of 'good' and 'bad,' and limit my vision. If I used the term 'good' on a thing, I'd lose my license to inspect it, because there might be bad in it ... I want to be able to look at the whole thing."

Of course, Doc Burton exemplifies "non-teleological" thinking, or "is" thinking, because he attempts to approach life with as much objectivity as possible. Just as a biologist does not want to create a parallax by intruding upon the subjects of his study, so the non-teleological writer does not want to compromise his material by intruding upon it. And later, Doc Burton attempts to explain the concept of "group-man" to Mac:

> I want to see, Mac. I want to watch these group-men, for they seem to me to be a new individual, not at all like single men. A man in a group isn't himself at all, he's a cell in an organism that isn't like him any more than the cells in your body are like you. I want to watch the group, and see what it's like ... Yes, it might be worth while to know more about group-man, to know his nature, his ends, his desires ... I simply want to see as much as I can, Mac.

Doc Burton's words thus exemplify the goal of the non-teleological thinker: "As [a] biologist he observes the 'animal' [i.e., a group of men acting as a single unit or animal] with scientific objectivity, hoping to discover in its behavior an order and a meaning within an ecological framework" (Marks, 18). Additionally, in other texts, Steinbeck portrays group-man without the scientific apparatus. For example, in "The Leader of the People," one of the short stories in *The Red Pony*, the grandfather describes the wagon train he led westward as group-man: "It wasn't Indians that were important, nor adventures, nor even getting out here. It was a whole bunch of people made into one big crawling beast. And I was the head. It was westering and westering. Every man wanted something for himself, but the big beast that was all of them wanted only westering."

In conclusion, the future of teaching and studying Steinbeck now lies in the balance—for despite Steinbeck's achievements and lifetime of productivity, critics have often panned his works. For example, although *The Grapes of Wrath* won the Pulitzer Prize in 1940, it was publicly burned by the St. Louis Public Library that same year, as well as being "barred from the Buffalo Public Library because 'vulgar words' were used,"[5] and it was challenged in California as questionable material.[6] Indeed, a compilation of six surveys conducted by U.S. librarians and libertarian organizations ranked *The Grapes of Wrath* among the ten "most frequently attacked books" in the U.S. since 1965.[7] And between 1990–1992, *The Grapes of Wrath* was the thirty-fourth most frequently challenged book in schools and libraries.[8]

In addition, one of Steinbeck's other achievements, *Of Mice and Men*, has fared even worse. Despite the fact that it was a smash on the page, stage, and big screen, copies of it were publicly burned at Oil City, Pennsylvania, in the 1970's,[9] and in the 1980's, the book was not only extracted from Ohio public schools, but it was also extirpated from Tennessee public schools, following a school board chairperson's promise "to remove all 'filthy books' from public school curricula and public libraries."[10] Between 1990–2000, in fact, *Of Mice and Men* was the sixth most frequently challenged book,[11] and in 2000, it was the fifth most-frequently challenged book.[12]

Nonetheless, Steinbeck, most likely, would not have been bothered by book-burning mobs banning his work. If anything, the visceral reaction his prose provoked testifies to the power of his art. If he hit a little too close to home and stepped on peoples' toes, he was only fulfilling the duties of a writer. According to his Nobel Prize Acceptance Speech, Steinbeck believed an artist was "charged with exposing our many grievous faults and failures, with dredging up to the light our dark and dangerous dreams for the purpose of improvement." Perhaps, then, Steinbeck succeeded in showing readers something about themselves they did not want to acknowledge, but must if they are to improve themselves. Could it be, for example, that Steinbeck held the mirror up to nature and showed human nature's tendency toward greediness or callousness?

Whether Steinbeck's work evokes commendations or condemnations, the furor over him has at least this going for it: it engenders curiosity. Moreover, it prompts speculation over what the future holds for Steinbeck studies. Critics are divided as to the future of *The Grapes of Wrath*, not only in and of itself, but also as the synecdoche—or the part representing the whole—of Steinbeck's corpus. In other words, the fate of *The Grapes of Wrath* is the perceived barometer thus measuring the fate of Steinbeck's other works. In one camp, Mary Brown finds that in American colleges and universities— justifiably—*The Grapes of Wrath* is being taught, and therefore being read, increasingly less frequently. Her research suggests that there are three primary reasons professors now rarely teach *The Grapes of Wrath*: first, some allege that "the book is simply not good (or not good enough to warrant inclusion in a course syllabus)"; second, others claim "the novel is dated and inappropriate for courses and students of the 90's";

and third, still others dismiss it because "the book is too long" (Brown, 287). For these reasons, Brown predicts that fewer and fewer people will teach or read the book as we move into the 21st century (297). She does hasten to note, though, that when students are assigned the text, they usually like it.

In another camp, critic Kenneth Swan finds reason after reason why Steinbeck still resonates with contemporary students. Certainly, when students study the novel, they often discover many "enduring values" with which they can share or identify. For example, "Steinbeck's ability to select an archetypal situation and shape it into his own story dramatizes the universality of human behavior and the cyclical recurrence of human situation and human responses" (Swan, 299, 300). For this reason, and others, Swan is much more optimistic about the future of *The Grapes of Wrath*: "as a parable of the strength and beauty of the human spirit, it achieves universal value. Such a story will always appeal to readers regardless of time, place, and relentless change" (307).

Critic James Gray, however, best captures the essence of Steinbeck's achievement, by comparing Steinbeck to F. Scott Fitzgerald:

> Steinbeck, for his inheritance, took the orchards and growing fields of California, the wasteland of the Depression, the refugee camps of rebels and the slums of poverty. He helped himself also to a scientific laboratory and certain places into which men retire to meditate. He, too, found pity and terror among his fellow human beings but, like Fitzgerald, he also found beauty, charm, and wit. Though the two never have thought of themselves as collaborators, they shared the responsibility to presenting in fiction all the conflicts that have confused our time and yet confirmed its aspirations. (Gray, 49)

NOTES

1. For more on Steinbeck and the stage, see Robert Morsberger, "Steinbeck and the Stage" in *The Short Novels of John Steinbeck: Critical Essays with a Checklist to Steinbeck Criticism*, ed. Jackson J. Benson (Durham, NC: Duke UP, 1990), pp. 271–314.

2. For more on Steinbeck and the big screen or television, see Robert Morsberger, *John Steinbeck: Zapata* (New York: Penguin, 1993).

3. For more, refer to Woodburn O. Ross' essay, "John Steinbeck: Naturalist's Priest." It appears in, among other places, *Steinbeck and His Critics: A Record of Twenty-Five Years*, edited by Tedlock and Wicker (Albuquerque: University of New Mexico Press, 1957) pp. 206–215.

4. When Steinbeck revised the *Sea of Cortez*, he removed the catalogue of their scientific findings, retained the journal he originally wrote (the "log") and which had originally appeared in *Sea of Cortez*, and then added a memoir of Ricketts, who had since died. This revised version is entitled *The Log from the Sea of Cortez* (1951).

5. www.ghs.bcsd.k12.il.us/projects/students/banned/grapes.htm

6. www.alibris.com/articles_features/features/banned/banned

7. http://www.thefileroon.org/fileroom/FileRoom/publication/ atkinshistory.html

8. www.-2.cs.cmu.edu/people/spok/most=banned.html

9. www.thefileroom.org/FileRoom/publication/atkinshistory.html

10. www.alibris.com/articles_features/features/banned/banned

11. www.ala.org./bbooks/top100bannednooks.html

12. www.ala.org.bbooks/challeng.html

WORKS CITED

Astro, Richard. *John Steinbeck and Edward F. Ricketts: The Shaping of a Novelist*. Minneapolis, MN: University of Minnesota Press, 1973.

Brown, Mary A. "*The Grapes of Wrath* and The Literary Canon of American Universities in the Nineties." *The Critical Response to John Steinbeck's* The Grapes of Wrath. Ed. Barbara A. Heavilin. CT: Greenwood Publishing Group, 2000.

Carpenter, Frederick I. "The Philosophical Joads." *Steinbeck and His Critics: A Record of Twenty-Five Year*s. Eds. Tedlock, E.W., Jr. and C.V. Wicker. Albuquerque, NM: Vol. of New Mexico Press, 1957.

DeMott, Robert, ed. *Working Days: The Journals of "The Grapes of Wrath."* New York: Viking, 1989.

Gladstein, Mimi R. *The Indestructible Woman in Faulkner, Hemingway, and Steinbeck*. Ann Arbor, MI: UMI Research Press, 1986.

Gray, James. "John Steinbeck: 1902–1968." *American Writers: A Collection of Literary Biographies*. Ed. Leonard Unger. Vol. 4. New York: Scribner's, 1974.

Kinney, Arthur F. "The Arthurian Cycle in *Tortilla Flat*." *Steinbeck: A Collection of Critical Essays*. Ed. Robert Murray Davis. Englewood Cliffs, NJ: Prentice-Hall, 1963.

Levant, Howard. *The Novels of John Steinbeck: A Critical Study*. Columbia, MO: University of Missouri Press, 1974.

Marks, Lester Jay. *Thematic Design in the Novels of John Steinbeck*. The Hague: Mouton, 1969.

Metzger, Charles R. "John Steinbeck's Paisano Knights." *Readings on John Steinbeck*, Ed. Clarice Swisher. San Diego, CA: Greenhaven Press, 1996.

———. "Steinbeck's Mexican-Americans." *Steinbeck: The Man and His Work*. Corvallis, OR: Oregon State UP, 1971.

Morsberger, Robert E. "Steinbeck and the Stage." *The Short Novels of John Steinbeck: Critical Essays with a Checklist to Steinbeck Criticism*, Ed. Jackson J. Benson. Durham, NC: Duke UP, 1990.

———,ed. *Zapata: A newly discovered narrative by John Steinbeck, with his screenplay of Viva Zapata!* New York: Penguin, 1993.

Ross, Woodburn O. "John Steinbeck: Naturalism's Priest." *Steinbeck and His Critics: A Record of Twenty Five Years*. Eds. Tedlock, E.W. Jr., and C.V. Wicker. Albuquerque, NM: University of New Mexico Press, 1957.

Shillinglaw, Susan. "John Steinbeck." *Encyclopedia of American Literature*, Ed. Steven R. Serafin. New York: Continuum, 1999.

Steinbeck, John. *The Acts of King Arthur and His Noble Knights*. Ed. Chase Horton. New York: Farrar, Strous & Giroux, 1976.

———. *America and Americans*. New York: Viking, 1966.

———. *Burning Bright*. New York: Viking, 1950.

———. *Canary Row*. New York: Viking, 1945.

———. *East of Eden*. New York: Viking, 1952.

———. *The Grapes of Wrath*. New York: Viking, 1939.

———. *In Dubious Battle*. New York: Covici-Friede, 1937.

———. *The Log From the "Sea of Cortez."* Viking, 1951.

————. *The Long Valley*. New York: Viking, 1938.

————. *Of Mice and Men*. New York: Covici-Friede, 1937.

————. "Nobel Peace Prize Acceptance Speech" (1962). *The Portable Steinbeck*. Ed. Pascal Covici. Revised and Enlarged Edition. New York: Penguin Books, 1976.

————. *Once There Was a War*. New York: Viking, 1958.

————. *The Red Pony*. New York: Covici-Friede, 1937.

————. *A Russian Journal*. New York: Viking, 1948.

————. *Sea of Cortez: A Leisurely Journal of Travel and Research*. New York: Viking, 1941.

————. *Their Blood Is Strong*. San Francisco: Samuel J. Lubin Society, 1938.

————. *Tortilla Flat*. New York: Covici-Friede, 1937.

————. *Travels with Charley, In Search of America*, New York: Viking, 1962

————. *Viva Zapata!* Ed. Robert E. Morseberger. New York: Viking, 1975.

————. *The Wayward Bus*. New York: Viking, 1947.

Swan, Kenneth. "The Enduring Values of John Steinbeck's Fiction: The University Student and *The Grapes of Wrath*." *The Critical Response to John Steinbeck's* The Grapes of Wrath. Ed. Barbara Heavilin. CT: Greenwood Publishing Group, 2000.

Timmerman, John H. *John Steinbeck's Fiction: The Aesthetics of the Road Taken*. Norman, OK: University of Oklahoma, 1986.

Wollenberg, Charles, ed. *John Steinbeck: The Harvest Gypsies*. Berkeley, CA: Heyday Books, 1988.

HOWARD LEVANT

The Fully Matured Art:
The Grapes of Wrath

The enormous contemporary social impact of *The Grapes of Wrath* can
encourage the slippery reasoning that condemns a period novel to die
with its period. But continuing sales and critical discussions suggest that
The Grapes of Wrath has outlived its directly reportorial ties to the
historical past; that it can be considered as an aesthetic object, a good or
a bad novel per se. In that light, the important consideration is the
relative harmony of its structure and materials.

The Grapes of Wrath is an attempted prose epic, a summation of
national experience at a given time. Evaluation proceeds from that
identification of genre. A negative critical trend asserts that *The Grapes
of Wrath* is too flawed to command serious attention: the materials are
local and temporary, not universal and permanent; the conception of life
is overly simple; the characters are superficial types (except, perhaps, Ma
Joad); the language is folksy or strained by turns; and, in particular, the
incoherent structure is the weakest point—the story breaks in half, the
nonorganic, editorializing interchapters force unearned general
conclusions, and the ending is inconclusive as well as overwrought and
sentimental. The positive trend asserts that *The Grapes of Wrath* is a great
novel. Its materials are properly universalized in specific detail; the
conception is philosophical, the characters are warmly felt and deeply
created; the language is functional, varied, and superb on the whole; and

the structure is an almost perfect combination of the dramatic and the panoramic in sufficient harmony with the materials. This criticism admits that overwrought idealistic passages as well as propagandistic simplifications turn up on occasion, but these are minor flaws in an achievement on an extraordinary scale. Relatively detached studies of Steinbeck's ideas comprise a third trend. These studies are not directly useful in analytical criticism; they do establish that Steinbeck's social ideas are ordered and legitimate extensions of biological fact, hence scientific and true rather than mistaken or sentimental.

The two evaluative positions are remarkable in their opposition. They are perhaps overly simple in asserting that *The Grapes of Wrath* is either a classic of our literature or a formless pandering to sentimental popular taste. Certainly these extremes are mistaken in implying (when they do) that, somehow, *The Grapes of Wrath* is sui generis in relation to Steinbeck's work.

Trends so awkwardly triple need to be brought into a sharper focus. By way of a recapitulation in focus, consider a few words of outright praise:

> For all of its sprawling asides and extravagances, *The Grapes of Wrath* is a big book, a great book, and one of maybe two or three American novels in a class with *Huckleberry Finn*.

Freeman Champney's praise is conventional enough to pass unquestioned if one admires *The Grapes of Wrath*, or, if one does not, it can seem an invidious borrowing of prestige, shrilly emotive at that. Afterthought emphasizes the serious qualification of the very high praise. Just how much damage is wrought by those "sprawling asides and extravagances," and does *The Grapes of Wrath* survive its structural faults as *Huckleberry Finn* does, by virtue of its mythology, its characterization, its language? If the answers remain obscure, illumination may increase (permitting, as well, a clearer definition of the aesthetic efficacy of Steinbeck's ideas) when the context of critical discussion is the relationship of the novel's structure to materials.

Steinbeck's serious intentions and his artistic honesty are not in question. He had studied and experienced the materials intensely over a period of time. After a false start that he rejected (*L'Affaire Lettuceburg*), his conscious intention was to create an important literary work rather than a propagandistic shocker or a journalistic statement of the topical problem of how certain people faced one aspect of the Great Depression. Therefore, it is an insult to Steinbeck's aims to suggest that somehow *The Grapes of Wrath* is imperfect art but a "big" or "great" novel nevertheless. In all critical justice, *The Grapes of Wrath* must stand or fall as a serious and important work of art.

The consciously functional aspect of Steinbeck's intentions—his working of the materials—is clarified by a comparison of *The Grapes of Wrath* with *In Dubious Battle*. Both novels deal with labor problems peculiar to California, but that similarity cannot be pushed too far. The Joads are fruit pickers in California, but not of apples, the fruit mentioned in *In Dubious Battle*. The Joads pick cotton, and in the strike novel the people expect to move on to cotton. The Joads become involved in a strike but as strikebreakers rather than as strikers. Attitudes are less easy to camouflage. The strikers in *In Dubious Battle* and the Okies in *The Grapes of Wrath* are presented with sympathy whereas the owning class and much of the middle class have no saving virtue. The sharpest similarity is that both the strikers and the Okies derive a consciousness of the need for group action from their experiences; but even here there is a difference in emphasis. The conflict of interest is more pointed and the lessons of experience are less ambiguous in *The Grapes of Wrath* than in *In Dubious Battle*. The fact is that the two novels are not similar beyond a common basis in California labor problems, and Steinbeck differentiates that basis carefully in most specific details. The really significant factor is that different structures are appropriate to each novel. The restricted scope of *In Dubious Battle* demands a dramatic structure with some panoramic elements as they are needed. The broad scope of *The Grapes of Wrath* demands a panoramic structure; the dramatic elements appear as they are needed. Therefore, in each case, the primary critical concern must be the adequacy of the use of the materials, not the materials in themselves.

Steinbeck's profound respect for the materials of *The Grapes of Wrath* is recorded in a remarkable letter in which he explained to his literary agents and to his publisher the main reason for his withdrawing *L'Affaire Lettuceburg*, the hurried, propagandistic, thirty-thousand-word manuscript novel that preceded *The Grapes of Wrath*:

> I know I promised this book to you, and that I am breaking a promise in withholding it. But I had got smart and cagey

you see. I had forgotten that I hadn't learned to write books, that I will never learn to write them. A book must be a life that lives all of itself and this one doesn't do that. You can't write a book. It isn't that simple. The process is more painful than that. And this book is fairly clever, has skillful passages, but tricks and jokes. Sometimes I, the writer, seem a hell of a smart guy—just twisting this people out of shape. But the hell with it. I beat poverty for a good many years and I'll be damned if I'll go down at the first little whiff of success. I hope you, Pat, don't think I've double-crossed you. In the long run to let this book out would be to double-cross you. But to let the bars down is like a first theft. It's hard to do, but the second time it isn't so hard and pretty soon it is easy. If I should write three books like this and let them out, I would forget there were any other kinds.

This is Steinbeck's declaration of artistic purpose—and his effort to exorcise a dangerous (and permanent) aspect of his craft. Much of the motivation for Steinbeck's career is stated in this letter. After all, he did write *L'Affaire Lettuceburg*; and "tricks and jokes," detached episodes, and detached ironic hits, as well as a twisting of characters, are evident enough in much of Steinbeck's earlier work. But the depression materials were too serious to treat lightly or abstractly, or to subject to an imposed structure (mistaken idealism, nature worship, a metaphysical curse, a literary parallel). Such materials need to be in harmony with an appropriate structure.

From that intentional perspective, the central artistic problem is to present the universal and epical in terms of the individual and particular. Steinbeck chooses to deal with this by creating an individual, particular image of the epical experience of the dispossessed Okies by focusing a sustained attention on the experience of the Joads. The result is an organic combination of structures. Dramatic structure suits the family's particular history; panoramic structure proves out the representative nature of their history. To avoid a forced and artificial "typing," to assure that extensions of particular detail are genuinely organic, Steinbeck postulates a conceptual theme that orders structure and materials: the transformation of the Joad family from a self-contained, self-sustaining unit to a conscious part of a group, a whole larger than its parts. This thematic ordering is not merely implicit or ironic, as it is in *The Pastures of Heaven*, or withheld to create mystery as in *Cup of Gold* or *To a God Unknown*. Steinbeck chances the strength of the materials and the organic quality of their structure. And he defines differences: the group is not group-man. The earlier concept is a "beast," created by raw emotion ("blood"), short-lived, unwieldy, unpredictable, mindless; a monster that produces indiscriminate good or evil. The group is quite different—rational, stable, relatively calm—because it is an assemblage of like-minded people who retain their individual and traditional sense of right and wrong as a natural fact. Group-man lacks a moral dimension; the group is a morally pure instrument of power. The difference is acute at the level of leadership. The leaders have ambiguous aims in *In Dubious Battle*, but they are Christ-like (Jim Casy) or attain moral insight (Tom Joad) in *The Grapes of Wrath*.

The Grapes of Wrath is optimistic; *In Dubious Battle* is not. That the living part of the Joad family survives, though on the edge of survival, is less than glowingly optimistic, but that survival produces a mood that differs considerably from the unrelenting misery of *In Dubious Battle*. Optimism stems from the theme, most openly in the alternation of narrative chapter and editorial interchapter. While the Joads move slowly and painfully toward acceptance of the group, many of the interchapters define the broad necessity of that acceptance. Arbitrary plotting does not produce this change. Its development is localized in Ma Joad's intense focus on the family's desire to remain a unit; her recognition of the group is the dramatic resolution. ("Use' ta be the fambly was fust. It ain't so now. It's anybody. Worse off we get, the more we got to do.") Optimism is demonstrated also in experience that toughens, educates, and enlarges the stronger Joads in a natural process. On the simplest, crudest level, the family's journey and ordeal is a circumstantial narrative of an effort to reach for the good material life. Yet that is not the sole motive, and those members who have only that motive leave the family. On a deeper level, the family is attempting to rediscover the identity it lost when it was dispossessed; so the Joads travel from order (their old, traditional life) through disorder (the road, California) to some hope of a better, rediscovered order, which they reach in Ma's recognition and Tom's dedication. Their journey toward order is the ultimate optimistic, ennobling process, the earned, thematic resolution of the novel.

I do not intend to imply that Steinbeck pretties his materials. He does not stint the details of the family's various privations, its continual losses of dignity, and the death or disappearance of many of its members. On the larger scale, there is considerable objective documentation of the general economic causes of such misery—a circumstantial process that lifts *The Grapes of Wrath* out of the merely historic genre of the proletarian novel. Optimism survives as the ultimate value because of the will of the people to understand and to control the conditions of their lives despite constant discouragement.

This value is essentially abstract, political. Steinbeck deepens and universalizes it by developing the relationship between the family unit and "the people." The family is made up of unique individuals. "The people" embraces a timeless entity, a continuing past, present, and future of collective memory—but free of any social or political function. Time lag confounds the usefulness of "the people" as a guide for the present. The Joads and others like them know they may keep the land or get new land if they can kill or control "the Bank," as the old people killed Indians to take the land and controlled nature to keep it. But "the Bank" is more complicated an enemy than Indians or nature because it is an abstraction. (That buccaneering capitalism is an abstract or allegorical monster of evil is left to implication in *In Dubious Battle*. Steinbeck is far more directly allegorical in characterizing "the Bank" as an evil, nonhuman monster. Consequently there is, I think, a gain in horror but a relative loss of credibility.) So the Okies submit to dispossession in Oklahoma (forced by mechanized cheaper production of cotton) and to the huge migration into California (encouraged by landowners to get cheap field labor), motivated by the time lag that confuses them, for none of them comprehends the monstrous logic of modern economics. Despite their ignorance, in a process that is unifying in itself and is second only to survival, the families work at some way of preventing against "the Bank." The older, agrarian concept of "the people" is succeeded in time by the new concept of the group, an instrument of technology and political power—an analogue that works. Steinbeck makes this succession appear necessary and legitimate by a representation that excludes alternate solutions. The permitted solution seems a natural evolution, from people to group, because it is a tactic, not a fundamental change in folkways. Its process is long and painful because the emotive entity, "the people," needs to feel its way toward redefinition as the group—the abstract, political entity which emerges as an organic, particularized whole. This is brilliant literary strategy, in its grasp of operative metaphor and its avoidance of an overly obvious, loaded opposition. Steinbeck is scrupulously careful to keep to precise and exact circumstantial detail in this developed metaphor. Concretely, the panicky violence of "the Bank" is the reverse of the fact that (seemingly by habit) the Joads are kind to those who need their help and neighborly to people who are like them. The metaphor is persuasive.

Steinbeck is quite as scrupulous in the use of allegory as a way of universalizing an abstract particular. In his earlier work this method can produce a tangibly artificial, forced result, but allegory is a credible and functional device in *The Grapes of Wrath*. The turtle episode in chapter 3 is justly famous. Objectively, we have a fully realized description of a land turtle's patient, difficult journey over dust fields, across a road and walled embankment, and on through the dust. The facts are the starting point; nature is not distorted or manipulated to yield allegorical meaning. The turtle seems awkward but it is able to survive, like the Joads, and like them it is moving southwest, out of the dry area. It can protect itself against a natural danger like the red ant it kills, as the Joads protect themselves by their unity. The turtle's eyes are "fierce, humorous," suggesting force that takes itself easily; the stronger Joads are a fierce, humorous people. When mismanaged human power attacks, as when a truck swerves to hit the turtle, luck is on the animal's side—it survives by luck. The Joads survive the mismanagement that produced the Dust Bowl and the brutalizing man-made conditions in California as much by luck as by design. The relation to the Joads of the life-bearing function of the turtle is more obscure, or perhaps overly ambitious. The factual starting point is that, unknowingly, the turtle carries an oat seed in its shell and unknowingly drops and plants the seed in the dust, where it will rest until water returns. The most obvious link in the Joad family is the pregnant Rose of Sharon, but her baby is born dead. Perhaps compassion is "born," as in Uncle John's thoughts as he floats the dead baby down the flooding river in its apple box coffin: "Go down an' tell 'em. Go down in the street an' rot an' tell 'em that way. That's the way you can talk.... Maybe they'll know then." (The reversal of values is evident in the reversed symbolism; the river bears death—not life, the coffin—not water to seeds in the earth.) But this appeal is strained, too greatly distanced from the factual starting point. The link works in the restricted sense that Ruthie and Winfield are "planted," and will perhaps take root, in the new environment of California. At this point the careful allegory collapses under its own weight, yet care is taken to join the device to the central narrative. In chapter 4, Tom Joad picks up a turtle, and later Casy remarks on the tenacity of the breed:

> "Nobody can't keep a turtle though. They work at it and work at it, and at last one day they get out and away they go—off somewheres."

This recognition of the turtle's purposeful tenacity interprets and places the preceding interchapter in the central narrative. Tom calls the turtle "an old bulldozer," a figure that works in opposition to the threatening insect life the tractors suggest as self-defeating, destructive tools of "the Bank." Again, a purposeful turtle is opposed to homeless domestic animals, like the "thick-furred yellow shepherd dog" that passes Tom and Casy, to suggest precisely the ruined land and the destruction of the old ways of life on the most basic, animal level, where the wild (or free) animal survives best. These and other supporting details extend the exemplum into the narrative; they continue and deepen Steinbeck's foreshadowing, moralizing insight naturally, within the range of biological imagery. It is true, allowing for the one collapse of the allegory, that none of Steinbeck's earlier work exhibits as profound a comprehension of what can be done to "place" an allegorical narrative device.

The turtle interchapter is masterful enough. Steinbeck does even more with an extended instance of allegorizing—the introduction of the lapsed preacher, Jim Casy, into the Joad family. Casy has a role that is difficult to present within the limits of credibility. Casy may look too much like his function, the Christ-like force that impels the family toward its transformation into the group. If the novel is to have more significance than a reportorial narrative of travel and hardship, Casy's spiritual insights are a necessary means of stating a convincing philosophical optimism. The technical difficulty is that Casy does not have a forthright narrative function. He drops out of the narrative for almost one hundred and fifty pages, although his presence continues through the Joads' wondering at times what had happened to him. When he reenters the novel, he is killed off within fifteen pages—

sacrificed for the group in accord with his Christ-like function, with a phrase that recalls Christ's last words. In spite of the obvious technical difficulty in handling such materials, Steinbeck realizes Casy as fully as any of the major Joads. Casy's struggle with himself to define "sin" to include the necessary facts of the natural world lends him a completely human aspect. He earns the right to make moral statements because he bases all judgments on his own experience. This earned right to "witness" serves to keep Casy human, yet it permits him to function as if he were an allegorical figure. This is a brilliant solution, and Casy is Steinbeck's most successful use of a functional allegorical figure in a major role. His narrative sharpness contrasts amazingly with the dim realization of Sir Henry Morgan or Joseph Wayne.

Even Casy's necessary distance is functional rather than arbitrary. He exists outside the narrative in the sense that he travels with the Joads but he is not a member of the family, and there is no danger of confusing his adventures with theirs. Further, by right of his nature and experience, he has the function of being the living moral conscience of "the people." He travels with the Joads to witness the ordeal of the Okies, to understand its causes, and to do what he can to help. Steinbeck's convincing final touch is that, at the end, Tom Joad aspires to Casy's role. In this shift, Steinbeck manipulates allegory, he does not submit to its rigid quality, for Tom is not like Casy. Tom is far more violent, more capable of anger; having been shown the way, however, he may be more successful as a practical missionary than Casy. One might say that if Casy is to be identified with Christ, the almost human god, Tom is to be identified with Saint Paul, the realistic, tough organizer. The allegorical link by which Tom is "converted" and assumes Casy's role is deeply realized and rich with significance, not simply because it is a technical necessity, but because it is a confirmation of Casy's reality as a man and a teacher. The parallels to Christ and Saint Paul would be only and technical facts if they were not realized so profoundly. The trivial fact that Casy has Christ's initials dims beside this more profound and sustained realization.

Function, not mere design, is as evident in the use of characterization to support and develop a conflict of opposed ideas— mainly a struggle between law and anarchy. The one idea postulates justice in a moral world of love and work, identified in the past with "the people" and in the present with the government camp and finally with the union movement, since these are the modern, institutional forms the group may take. The opposed idea postulates injustice in an immoral world of hatred and starvation. It is associated with buccaneering capitalism, which, in violent form, includes strikebreaking and related practices that cheapen human labor.

The Joads present special difficulties in characterization. They must be individualized to be credible and universalized to carry out their representative functions. Steinbeck meets these problems by making each of the Joads a specific individual and by specifying that what happens to the Joads is typical of the times. The means he uses to maintain these identities can be shown in some detail. The least important Joads are given highly specific tags—Grandma's religion, Grandpa's vigor, Uncle John's melancholy, and Al's love of cars and girls. The tags are involved in events; they are not inert labels. Grandma's burial violates her religion; Grandpa's vigor ends when he leaves the land; Uncle John's melancholy balances the family's experience; Al helps to drive the family to California and, by marrying, continues the family. Ma, Pa, Rose of Sharon, and Tom carry the narrative, so their individuality is defined by events rather than through events. Ma is the psychological and moral center of the family; Pa carries its burdens; Rose of Sharon means to ensure its physical continuity; and Tom becomes its moral conscience. On the larger scale, there is much evidence that what happens to the family is typical of the times. The interchapters pile up suggestions that "the whole country is moving" or about to move. The Joads meet many of their counterparts or outsiders who are in sympathy with their ordeal; these meetings reenforce the common bond of "the people." Both in the interchapters and the narrative, the universal, immediate issue is survival—a concrete universal.

On the other hand, the individualized credibility of the Joads is itself the source of two difficulties: the Joads are too different, as sharecroppers, to suggest a universal or even a national woe, and they speak an argot that might limit their universal quality. (It is a curious fact that Steinbeck attempts to create a so-called "universal language" in *Burning Bright*, a far more theory-ridden novel than *The Grapes of Wrath*. In any event, the attempt produces a fantastic, wholly incredible language.) Steinbeck handles these limitations with artistic license. The narrative background contains the Joads' past; their experience as a landless proletariat is highlighted in the narrative foreground. The argot is made to seem a typical language within the novel in three ways: it is the major language; people who are not Okies speak variations of their argot; and that argot is not specialized in its relevance, but is used to communicate the new experiences "the people" have in common as a landless proletariat. However, because these solutions depend on artistic license, any tonal falseness undermines severely the massive artistic truthfulness the language is intended to present. So the overly editorial tone in several of the interchapters has a profoundly false linguistic ring, although the tonal lapse is limited and fairly trivial in itself.

The Joads are characterized further in comparison with four Okie types who refuse to know or are unable to gain the knowledge the family derives from its collective experience. They are the stubborn, the dead, the weak, and the backtrackers; they appear in the novel in that order.

Muley Graves is the stubborn man, as his punning name suggests. He reveals himself to Tom and Casy near the beginning of the novel. His refusal to leave Oklahoma is mere stubbornness; his isolation drives him somewhat mad. He is aware of a loss of reality, of "jus' wanderin' aroun' like a damn ol' graveyard ghos'," and his blind violence is rejected from the beginning by the strongest, who oppose his pessimism with an essential optimism.

Deaths of the aged and the unborn frame the novel. Grandpa and Grandma are torn up by the roots and die, incapable of absorbing a new, terrible experience. Rose of Sharon's baby, born dead at the end of the novel, is an index of the family's ordeal and a somewhat contrived symbol of the necessity to form the group.

The weak include two extremes within the Joad family. Noah Joad gives up the struggle to survive; he finds a private peace. His character is shadowy, and his choice is directed more clearly by Steinbeck than by any substance within him. Connie has plenty of substance. He is married to Rose of Sharon and deserts her because he had no faith in the family's struggle to reach California. His faith is absorbed in the values of "the Bank," in getting on, in money, in any abstract goal. He wishes to learn about technology in order to rise in the world. He does not admire technique for itself, as Al does. He is a sexual performer, but he loves no one. Finally, he wishes that he had stayed behind in Oklahoma and taken a job driving a tractor. In short, with Connie, Steinbeck chooses brilliantly to place a "Bank" viewpoint within the family. By doing so, he precludes a simplification of character and situation, and he endorses the complexity of real people in the real world. (*In Dubious Battle* is similarly free of schematic characterization.) In addition, the family's tough, humanistic values gain in credibility by their contrast with Connie's shallow, destructive modernity. The confused gas station owner and the pathetic one-eyed junkyard helper are embodied variations on Connie's kind of weakness. Al provides an important counterpoint. He wants to leave the family at last, like Connie, but duty and love force him to stay. His hard choice points the moral survival of the family and measures its human expense.

The Joads meet several backtrackers. The Wilsons go back because Mrs. Wilson is dying; the Joads do not stop, in spite of death. The ragged man's experience foreshadows what the Joads find in California; but they keep on. Some members of the Joad family think of leaving but do not, or they leave for specific reasons—a subtle variation on backtracking. Al and Uncle John wish deeply at times to leave, but they stay; Tom leaves (as Casy does) but to serve the larger, universal family of the group. Backtracking is a metaphor, then, a denial of life, but always a fact as well. The factual metaphor is deepened into complexity because the Joads sympathize with the backtrackers' failure to endure the hardships of the road and of California, in balance with where they started from—the wasteland—while knowing they cannot accept that life-denying solution. All of these choices are the fruit of the family's experience.

A fifth group of owners and middle-class people are accorded no sympathetic comprehension, as contrasted with the Joads, and, as in *In Dubious Battle*, their simply and purely monstrous characterization is too abstract to be fully credible. The few exceptions occur in highly individualized scenes or episodes (chapter 15 is an example) in which middle-class "shitheels" are caricatures of the bad guys, limited to a broad contrast with the good guys (the truck drivers, the cook), who are in sympathy with a family of Okies. (Fifteen years later, Steinbeck detailed this technique in a witty article, "How to Tell Good Guys from Bad Guys," *The Reporter* 12 [March 10, 1955], 42–44. In that quite different, political context, Steinbeck demonstrates that he knows the technique is too bluntly black and white to permit any but the broadest cartoon characterization. There is every reason to think he knew as much in 1935 or 1939.) This limitation has the narrative advantage of highlighting the importance and vitality of the Okies to the extent that they seem by right to belong in the context of epic materials, but the disadvantage of shallow characterization is severe. Steinbeck can provide a convincing detailed background of the conditions of the time; he cannot similarly give a rounded, convincing characterization to an owner or a disagreeable middle-class person.

On the whole, then, fictive strength and conviction are inherent in the materials of *The Grapes of Wrath*. The noticeable flaws are probably irreducible aspects of the time context and of narrative shorthand, counterpointed by a complex recognition of human variety in language and behavior.

The ordering of the structure supports this conclusion. *The Grapes of Wrath* has three parts: Tom's return and his witnessing of events; the family's departure and experiences on the road; its arrival and experiences in California. The interchapters "locate" and generalize the narrative chapters, somewhat like stage directions. They supply, in a suitably dramatic or rhetorical style, information the Joads cannot possess, and they are involved more often than not in the narrative. (Because of that involvement, it is incorrect to think of the interchapters as choral. We see the difference in comparing the four detached interchapters in *Cup of Gold* with any interchapters in *The Grapes of Wrath*, and we see as well Steinbeck's artistic growth in the organic integration of chapter and interchapter in the later novel. The stylistic variety always suited to its content is further evidence of a conscious, intentional artistry.) This device provides for both precise detail and epic scope. The imagery fulfills the structural purpose of pitting life against death.

The first part contains ten chapters. The opening is a "location" interchapter. The dead land of the Dust Bowl in Oklahoma provides the imagery of a universal death, but at the close the women watch their men to see if they will break in the stress of that natural disaster. The men do not break; the scene is repeated in California at the close of the novel in a rising rhetoric. The objective imagistic frame sets life against death, and life endures in the will of the people to endure. The following nine chapters center on Tom's return from a kind of death—prison. With Casy, Tom is an external observer, witnessing with fresh eyes the dead land and the universal dispossession. Death seems to prevail. The turtle interchapter is recapitulated ironically in the narrative. Pa carries handbills that promise jobs in California, an analogue to the turtle carrying a head of oats; but the handbills falsely promise renewal; their intention is to cheapen the labor market. Later events prove the group concept is the genuine renewal, the true goal. Immediately, death is associated with "the Bank," an abstraction presented concretely in symbolic form as the tractor—the perfect tool of the abstract "Bank," which dehumanizes its driver and kills the fertility of the land.

When he sees the abandoned Joad home, Tom says, "Maybe they're all dead," but Muley Graves tells Tom the family is alive, with Uncle John, and about to leave without him for California. Tom is reborn or returned to life within the family, but its vital center has shifted (as represented in charged, frankly mystical terms) to a life-giving machine:

> The family met at the most important place, near the truck.
> The house was dead, and the fields were dead; but this truck
> was the active thing, the living principle.

The family's certainties develop from an ironically hopeful innocence, a failure to realize that a new basis for life has overtaken them, replacing family with group. The trek is an instinctive flight from death, but the economic system is more deadly than the drough. The Joads accept the promise of the handbills, they are cheated when they sell their farm equipment, but they do not doubt that they will transplant themselves in California. The real certainty is the death of the past, as in the burning of relics by an unnamed woman in an interchapter, and by Ma herself, just before the trek begins.

All that is not dead is altered. Pa's loss of authority to Ma and Al's new authority (he knows automobiles) represent the shifts in value within the family. They retain a living coherence as farmers. They work as a unit when they kill and salt down the hogs in preparation for the trek. They are innocent of the disgusting techniques of close dealing in business, but Tom explains to Casy how the Joads can deal closely enough in their accustomed agrarian context. Their innocence, therefore, is touching, not comic, and their literal preparations support a symbolic preparation, a blindly hopeful striving to find life. Their journey is an expression, despite all shocks and changes, of the will to survive; hence, it has an epic dignity, echoing their retained, personal dignity.

In all the imagery of life and death, Steinbeck is consistent in that his symbols grow out of objective, literal facts. He thus achieves imagery in a more fully realized texture in this novel than in earlier work. This organically realized symbolism is maintained and developed in the seven chapters of the second section.

With the dead land behind them, the family carries the death of the past on its journey. Grandpa dies on the first night. Probably his stroke is caused, at least in part, by the "medicine" that Ma and Tom dope him with to take him away from the land—for the good of the family as a whole. An incipient group concept emerges in this overriding concern for the whole. Grandpa's death is offset by the meeting of the Joads and the Wilsons. At the beginning, Grandpa's illness and death join the two families in bonds of sympathy. There are other unifying forces; the language bar becomes senseless, and the two families help each other. Casy sees the emergence of the group, the whole absorbing the individual, in his sermon for Grandpa:

> Casy said solemnly, "This here ol' man jus' lived a life an' jus' died out of it. I don't know whether he was good or bad, but that don't matter much. He was alive, an' that's what matters. An' now he's dead, an' that don't matter. Heard a fella tell a poem one time, an' he says, 'All that lives is holy.'"

A modest dignity embodies the vitalistic dogma. As a further push from individual to group, the family decides to break the law by burying Grandpa secretly beside the road; a conventional funeral would eat up the money they need to reach California. Grandma's grisly, circumstantial death is delayed until the end of the section; it outweighs the achievement of reaching their destination and foreshadows the reality of California. True, the family can absorb death, even new kinds of death, into its experience. Ruthie and Winfield react most violently to the dog's death at the first stop on the road; they are less affected by Grandpa's death, still less by Grandma's. Late on the night of Grandpa's death after the Joads and Wilsons have agreed to join forces, Ma remarks: "Grandpa—it's like he's dead a year." Experience breeds a calm in the face of loss that fills in the past. Tom points this harshly realistic network of difference after Grandma's death:

"They was too old," he said. "They wouldn't of saw nothin' that's here. Grampa would a been a-seein' the Injuns an' the prairie country when he was a young fella. An' Granma would a remembered an' seen the first home she lived in. They was too ol'. Who's really seein' it is Ruthie and Winfiel'."

Life matters. The narrative context supports this fruit of the family's private experience. Between the deaths of Grandpa and Grandma, the Joads meet several symbolically dead people on the road. The gas station owner is incapable of learning the meaning of his own experience even when it is explained to him. The one-eyed junkyard helper lives in a prison of self, inside his ugly face and unclean body. Tom (who was in an actual prison) tries unsuccessfully to force him from his death into life. The several returning sharecroppers have come to accept a living death as the only reality. They have cut themselves off from the inchoate struggle to form a group, admittedly against severe odds, so they have no choice but to return to the dead, empty land.

But to outsiders, seeing only the surface, the Joads are not heroic lifebearers but stupidly ignorant, as in a dialogue between two service station boys when the family leaves on the final lap of the trek, the night trip across the Mojave Desert:

"Jesus, I'd hate to start out in a jalopy like that." "Well, you and me got sense. Them goddamn Okies got no sense and no feeling. They ain't human. A human being wouldn't live like they do. A human being couldn't stand to be so dirty and miserable. They ain't a hell of a lot better than gorillas." "Just the same. I'm glad I ain't crossing the desert in no Hudson Super-Six...." "You know, they don't have much trouble. They're so goddamn dumb they don't know it's dangerous. And, Christ Almighty, they don't know any better than what they got. Why worry?"

The dialogue is exactly true, but the truth is ironic. The Joads do have the appearance of death, and ignorant, dirty, dispossessed yokels seem to be unlikely carriers of an affirmation of life. The ironic truth defines the heroism of the Joads. The family is aware of the dangers of the desert crossing, and Grandma dies during it, "for the fambly," as Ma says. In general the family is more aware than the boys at the service station are allowed to know. After meeting a second returning sharecropper, the Joads are even aware of the actual conditions in California; Uncle John, the family's weakest moral agent, voices the family's rejection of despair when he says, "We're a-goin' there, ain't we? None of this here talk gonna keep us from goin' there." The service station boys express, so we can dismiss, a superficially sentimental view of the Joads. The ironic truth is that the family goes ahead, knowing the dangers and aware that California may not be Eden. Their genuine heroism and nobility are all the more valid for being tested by irony.

Yet there is no suggestion that the Joads are merely deterministic formulae. They are pawns of circumstance up to a point. They react to events they do not understand fully, and no doubt partial ignorance and pure necessity keep them on the road and get them to California. But Ma and Tom undergo certain developments of character that exclude determinism. Ma's constantly increasing moral authority is her response to the forces that are tearing the family apart, but she acts out of love that is restricted to the family, that is not universalized until very near the end of the novel. Tom's role is more extensive and more complex. He begins by regarding himself as a creature of necessity—"I ruther jus' lay one foot down in front a the other"—but his quietism relates to a prison experience he does not want to live "over an' over." His natural understanding of why and how people behave forces him into a moral concern that is larger but as intense as Ma's. His knowledge of people is established at the beginning of the novel, in his shrewd, unflattering understanding of the truck driver who gives him a lift, and it widens subsequently with experience on the road. His disdain for the gas station owner precedes his tough moral lecture to the one-eyed junkyard helper and an equally tough lecture to Al. That is to say, Tom is involved. His moral development follows Casy's, with the significant difference that his is the more difficult to achieve. Casy is a relatively simple character; he can express moral concern easily. Tom's emotional numbness following his time in prison does not permit meditation or cancel personality, so the awakening of his moral consciousness on the road is a more rigorous, more painful experience than Casy's time in the desert. Consequently, because of its special quality, Tom's growing awareness of good and evil is a highly credible mirror of the general experience that drives the family toward the group. The logic is paradoxical, but the artistic insight is realized deeply in Tom's circumstantial journey from moral quietism to moral concern for the group.

Enduring all the harsh experiences of their journey, the family gains moral stature and finds that it can function as a unit in the new environment of the road. Its survival in California is a result in part of its redefinition gained on the road.

The interchapters underscore and generalize these particulars. Chapter 14 states the growth of the group concept as a shift in the thinking of the migrants from *I* to *we*. The narrative context is Grandpa's death and the unity of the Joads and Wilsons. Chapter 15 suggests that the Joads' ordeal is a moral experience that affects society at large. Chapter 17 continues the theme that the road furthers the growth of the group concept:

> Every night relationships that make a world, established; every morning the world torn down like a circus. At first the families were timid in the building and tumbling worlds, but gradually the technique of building worlds became their technique. Then leaders emerged, then laws were made, then codes came into being. And as the worlds moved westward they were more complete and better furnished, for their builders were more experienced in building them.

The formation of a group is a "technique" with its basis in the older agrarian order. As with the Joads, the experience of building produces a new moral stature and a redefinition of the family.

In the relation of these events and changes, the narrative chapters and interchapters cohere in an organic unity. Their common theme is movement from and through death to a new life inherent in the group concept. The symbolic level extends the narrative level of movement on the road through time and space. The texture is fully realized. No generalization violates narrative particulars or exists apart from them. Steinbeck's work is careful, convincing, flawless.

The third part—the family's arrival and experience in California— marks an artistic decline. The materials alter and at times the structure is defective.

The chief difference in the materials is an absolute focus on man- made misery. In Oklahoma and on the road, survival can seem to be mainly a struggle against natural conditions. Drouth is the cause of the migration. "The Bank" dispossesses the Okies, but it is not the effective cause of the drouth. In California the struggle is almost entirely against men, and there is no possibility of an escape by further migration. The chief difference in structure stems from Steinbeck's need to begin to think of how to conclude the novel, which presents structural choices and manipulations not present in the first two parts of the novel. For a time the narrative thrust remains coherent, an organic unity disguising these changes.

Grandma's undignified burial establishes the pattern of the family's experience in California. Her pauper's funeral by the state contrasts with the full dignity and free will the family expressed in burying Grandpa. Landless poverty is a moral insult to family pride, and it affects their will to survive. For the moment, as their moral spokesman, Ma expresses a will to recover as quickly as possible for the sake of the future:

> "We got to git," she said. "We got to find a place to stay. We got to get to work an' settle down. No use a-lettin' the little fellas go hungry. That wasn't never Granma's way. She always et a good meal at a funeral."

The conserving lesson of the past is negated by the present economic reality. Ma's brave gesture fails as the family learns that California is a false goal. The imagery associated with California indicates these negations. Peter Lisca and Joseph Fontenrose have pointed to the major biblical parallels in *The Grapes of Wrath*, including those associating California and the Promised Land. The parallels are intensive, even more so than Lisca and Fontenrose suggest, and their function is ironic rather than associative. To begin with, California evokes images of plenty to eat and drink. The ironic fact is that California is the literal reverse of Canaan; there is little to eat and drink, at least for Okies; but California is the Promised Land so far as the family's experience there forces the full emergence of the group concept. Appropriately, the family enters California with a foreboding that runs counter to their expectations:

> Pa called, "We're here—we're in California!" They looked dully at the broken rock glaring under the sun, and across the river the terrible ramparts of Arizona.

They have crossed over, but the physical imagery foreshadows their actual human environment. The land is green across the river, but the biblical lists of landscape features are framed by the fact that they have been carrying Grandma's corpse. The human reality of California life is a living death, as the first camp, the Hooverville, suggests: "About the camp there hung a slovenly despair," everything is "grey" and "dirty," there is no work, no food, and no evident means of overcoming "despair." The deadly economic reality is explained by a young man in the Hooverville, when Tom asks why the police "shove along" the migrants:

> "Some say they don' want us to vote; keep us movin' so we can't vote. An' some says so we can't get on relief. An' some says if we set in one place we'd get organized."

That reply announces the political solution, the humanly possible way of countervailing power through organization. But the words are programmatic, not a revelation of character.

The difference in materials and in structure begins to appear at this point. The root of the matter is that Steinbeck is so compelled by the documentary facts that he permits their narration to take precedence over the central theme of the family's transformation into the group. And in moving the novel toward an affirmation of life in response to the facts, Steinbeck allows the Joads' experience in California to become a series of allegorical details within a panoramic structure. The narrowed scope of the materials and the schematic handling of the structure are visible in nearly every event in this part of the novel.

Casy's alternative to "despair," sacrificing himself for "the people," is almost wholly an allegorical solution. It is so abstractly schematic that at first none of the family understands its meaningful allegorical force—that loss of self leads to the group concept and thus to power to enforce the will of the group. Instead, the narrative is largely an account of the family's efforts to avoid starvation. The phrase "We got to eat" echoes through these concluding chapters. Ma's changing attitude toward hungry unknown children is ambiguous: "I dunno what to do. I can't rob the fambly. I got to feed the fambly." Ma grows more positive, later, when she is nagged by a storekeeper in the struck orchard:

"Any reason you got to make fun? That help you any?" "A fella got to eat," he began; and then, belligerantly, "A fella got a right to eat." "What fella?" Ma asked.

Ma asserts finally that only "the poor" constitute a group that practices charity:

> "I'm learnin' one thing good," she said. "Learnin' it all a time, ever' day. If you're in trouble or hurt or need—go to poor people. They're the only ones that'll help—the only ones."

"The poor" are identified with "the people," who, in turn are the emerging group. Their purity is allegorical, and, in its limitation, incredible. Steinbeck's handling of "the poor" in *In Dubious Battle* is much less schematic, and therefore far more credible. In general, romanticizing "the poor" is more successful in an outright fantasy like *Tortilla Flat* but Steinbeck commits himself to a measure of realism in *The Grapes of Wrath* that does not sort well with the allegorical division of "good" from "evil."

Romanticizing "the poor" extends beyond Ma's insight to an idealization of the "folk law" that Tom envisions as the fruit of his own experience in California—at a great distance from the "building" experience on the road:

> "I been thinkin' how it was in that gov'ment camp, how our folks took care a theirselves, an' if they was a fight they fixed it theirself; an' they wasn't no cops wagglin' their guns, but they was better order than them cops ever give. I been a-wonderin' why we can't do that all over. Throw out the cops that ain't our people. All work together for our own thing—all farm our own lan'."

Presenting the reverse of Tom's beatific vision in an interchapter, Steinbeck draws on the imagery of the novel's title:

> This vineyard will belong to the bank. Only the great owners can survive.... Men who can graft the trees and make the seed

fertile and big can find no way to let the hungry people eat their produce.... In the souls of the people the grapes of wrath are filling and growing heavy, growing heavy for the vintage.

It is not vitally important that Steinbeck's prediction of some kind of agrarian revolt has turned out to be wrong. The important artistic fact is that "good," divided sharply, abstractly, from "evil," argues that Steinbeck is not interested in rendering the materials in any great depth. Consider the contrast between the people in the government camp and in the struck orchard. Point by point, the camp people are described as clean, friendly, joyful, and organized, while in the struck orchard they are dirty, suspicious, anxious, and disorganized by the police. Credibility gives way to neat opposites, which are less than convincing because Steinbeck's government camp is presented openly as a benevolent tyranny that averages out the will of "the people" to live in dignity and excludes people unable or unwilling to accept that average.

Neat opposites can gather fictive conviction if they are realized through individuals and in specific detail. There is something of that conviction in specific action against specific men, as when the camp leaders exclude troublemakers hired by business interests to break up the camp organization. There is more awkwardness in the exclusion of a small group of religious fanatics obsessed with sin. An important factor is that these people are genuinely Okies, not tools of the interests; another is that the exclusion is necessary, not realistic, if the secular values of the group concept are to prevail. Allowing for his selection and schematic treatment of these materials, Steinbeck does engineer his manipulated point with artistic skill. Fanaticism is considered a bad thing throughout the novel, both as a religious stance and as a social phenomenon. Tom's first meeting with Casy identifies "spirit" with emotional release, not a consciousness of sin, and Casy announces his own discovery, made during his time in the desert, of a social rather than an ethical connection between "spirit" and sexual excitement. Further, fanaticism is identified repeatedly with a coercive denial of life. Rose of Sharon is frightened, in the government camp, by a fanatic woman's argument that dancing is sinful, that it means Rose will lose her baby. The woman's ignorance is placed against the secular knowledge of the camp manager:

"I think the manager, he took [another girl who danced] away to drop her baby. He don' believe in sin.... Says the sin is bein' hungry. Says the sin is bein' cold."

She compounds ignorance by telling Ma that true religion demands fixed economic classes:

"[A preacher] says 'They's wicketness in that camp.' He says, 'The poor is tryin' to be rich.' He says, 'They's dancin' an' huggin' when they should be wailin' an' moanin' in sin.'"

These social and economic denials of life are rooted in ignorance, not in spiritual enlightenment, and they are countered by the materialistic humanism of the camp manager. So fanaticism is stripped of value and associated with business in its denial of life. The case is loaded further by the benevolent tyranny of the group. Fanatics are not punished for their opinions, or even for wrongdoing. They are merely excluded, or they exclude themselves.

A similar process is apparent in the group's control of social behavior, as when Ruthie behaves as a rugged individual in the course of a children's game:

The children laid their mallets on the ground and trooped silently off the court.... Defiantly she hit the ball again.... She pretended to have a good time. And the children stood and watched.... For a moment she stared at them, and then she flung down the mallet and ran crying for home. The children walked back on the court. Pig-tails said to Winfield, "You can git in the nex' game." The watching lady warned them, "When she comes back an' wants to be decent, you let her. You was mean yourself, Amy."

The punishment is directive. The children are being trained to accept the group and to become willing parts of the group. The process is an expression of "folk law" on a primary level. There is no doubt that Ruthie learned her correct place in the social body by invoking a suitably social punishment.

Perhaps the ugliness implicit in the tyranny of the group has become more visible lately. Certainly recent students of the phenomenon of modern conformity could supply Steinbeck with very little essential insight. The real trouble is precisely there. The tyranny of the group is visible in all of Steinbeck's instances (its ambiguity is most evident in Ruthie's case), which argues for Steinbeck's artistic honesty in rendering the materials. But he fails to see deeply enough, to see ugliness and ambiguity, because he has predetermined the absolute "good" of group behavior—an abstraction that precludes subtle technique and profound insight, on the order of Doc Burton's reservations concerning group-man. The result is a felt manipulation of values and a thinning of credibility.

Given this tendency, Steinbeck does not surprise us by dealing abstractly with the problem of leadership in the government camp. Since there is minimal narrative time in which to establish the moral purity of Jim Rawley, the camp manager, or of Ezra Huston, the chairman of the Central Committee, Steinbeck presents both men as allegorical figures. Particularly Jim Rawley. His introduction suggests his allegorical role. He is named only once, and thereafter he is called simply "the camp manager." His name is absorbed in his role as God. He is dressed "all in white," but he is not a remote God. "The frayed seams on his white coat" suggest his human availability, and his "warm" voice matches his social qualities. Nevertheless, there is no doubt that he is God visiting his charges:

> He put the cup on the box with the others, waved his hand, and walked down the line of tents. And Ma heard him speaking to the people as he went.

His identification with God is bulwarked when the fanatic woman calls him the devil:

> "She says you was the devil," [says Rose of Sharon]. "I know she does. That's because I won't let her make people miserable.... Don't you worry. She doesn't know."

What "she doesn't know" is everything the camp manager does know; and if he is not the devil, he must be God. But his very human, secular divinity—he can wish for an easier lot, and he is always tired from overwork—suggests the self-sacrifice that is Casy's function. The two men are outwardly similar. Both are clean and "lean as a picket," and the camp manager has "merry eyes" like Casy's when Tom meets Casy again. These resemblances would be trivial, except for a phrase that pulls them together and lends them considerable weight. Ezra Huston has no character to speak of, beyond his narrative function, except that when he has finished asking the men who try to begin a riot in the camp why they betrayed "their own people," he adds: "They don't know what they're doin'." This phrase foreshadows Casy's words to his murderer just before he is killed in an effort to break the strike: "You don't know what you're a-doin'." Just as these words associate Casy with Christ, so they associate the leaders in the government camp with Casy. Steinbeck's foreshortening indicates that, because Casy is established firmly as a "good" character, the leaders in the government camp must resemble Casy in that "good" identity.

The overall process is allegorical, permitting Steinbeck to assert that the camp manager and Ezra Huston are good men by definition and precluding the notion that leadership may be a corrupting role, as in *In Dubious Battle*. It follows that violence in the name of the group is "good," whereas it is "evil" in the name of business interests. The contrast is too neat, too sharp, to permit much final credibility in narrative or in characterization.

A still more extreme instance of Steinbeck's use of allegory is the process by which Tom Joad assumes the role of a leader. Tom's pastoral concept of the group is fully developed, and as the novel ends, Tom identifies himself through mystic insight with the group. Appropriately, Tom explains his insight to Ma because Tom's function is to act while Ma's function is to endure—in the name of the group. More closely, Ma's earlier phrase, "We're the people—we go on," is echoed directly in Tom's assurance when Ma fears for his life:

> "Well, maybe like Casy says, a fella ain't got a soul of his own, but on'y a piece of a big one—an' then—" "Then what, Tom?" "Then it don't matter. Then I'll be all aroun' in the dark. I'll be ever'where—wherever you look.... See? God, I'm talkin' like Casy. Comes of thinkin' about him so much. Seems like I can see him sometimes."

This anthropomorphic insight, borrowed from *To a God Unknown* and remotely from Emerson, is a serious idea, put seriously within the allegorical framework of the novel's close. Two structural difficulties result. First, Tom has learned more than Casy could have taught him— that identification with the group, rather than self-sacrifice *for* the group, is the truly effective way to kill the dehumanized "Bank." Here, it seems, the Christ/Casy, Saint Paul/Tom identifications were too interesting in themselves, for they limit Steinbeck's development of Tom's insight to a mechanical parallel, such as the suggestion that Tom's visions of Casy equate with Saint Paul's visions of Christ. Second, the connection between the good material life and Tom's mystical insight is missing. There is Steinbeck's close attention to Tom's political education and to his revival of belief in a moral world. But, in the specific instance, the only bridge is Tom's sudden feeling that mystical insight connects somehow with the good material life. More precisely, the bridge is Steinbeck's own assertion, since Tom's mystical vision of pastoral bliss enters the narrative only as an abstract announcement on Steinbeck's part.

Characterization is, as might be assumed, affected by this abstracting tendency. Earlier, major characters such as Tom and Ma are "given" through actions in which they are involved, not through detached, abstract essays; increasingly, at the close, the method of presentation is the detached essay or the extended, abstract speech. Steinbeck's earlier, more realized presentation of Tom as a natural man measures the difference. Even a late event, Tom's instinctive killing of Casy's murderer, connects organically with Tom's previous "social" crimes—the murder in self-defense, for which Tom has finished serving a prison term when the novel begins, and the parole that Tom jumps to go with the family to California. In all of these crimes, Tom's lack of guilt or shame links with the idea that "the people" have a "natural" right to unused land—not to add life, liberty, and the pursuit of happiness—and that "the Bank" has nothing but an abstract, merely legal right to such land. Tom's mystical vision is something else; it is a narrative shock, not due to Tom's "natural" responses, but to the oversimplified type of the "good" man that Tom is made to represent in order to close the novel on a high and optimistic note. Tom is a rather complex man earlier on, and the thinning out of his character, in its absolute identification with the "good," is an inevitable result of allegorizing.

Style suffers also from these pressures. Tom's speech has been condemned, as Emerson's writing never is, for mawkishness, for maudlin lushness, for the soft, rotten blur of intellectual evasion. Style is a concomitant of structure; its decline is an effect, not a cause. Tom's thinking is embarrassing, not as thought, but as the stylistic measure of a process of manipulation that is necessary to close the novel on Steinbeck's terms.

The final scene, in which Rose of Sharon breastfeeds a sick man, has been regarded universally as the nadir of bad Steinbeck, yet the scene is no more or no less allegorical than earlier scenes in this final part. Purely in a formal sense, it parallels Tom's mystical union or identification with the group: it affirms that "life" has become more important than "family" in a specific action, and, as such, it denotes the emergence of the group concept. In that light, the scene is a technical accomplishment. Yet it is a disaster from the outset, not simply because it is sentimental; its execution, through the leading assumption, is incredible. Rose of Sharon is supposed to become Ma's alter ego by taking on her burden of moral insight, which, in turn, is similar to the insight that Tom reaches. There is no preparation for Rose of Sharon's transformation and no literary justification except a merely formal symmetry that makes it desirable, in spite of credibility, to devise a repetition. Tom, like Ma, undergoes a long process of education; Rose of Sharon is characterized in detail throughout the novel as a protected, rather thoughtless, whining girl. Possibly her miscarriage produces an unmentioned, certainly mystical change in character. More likely the reader will notice the hand of the author, forcing Rose of Sharon into an unprepared and purely formalistic role.

Once given this degree of manipulation, direct sentimentality is no surprise. Worse, the imagistic shift from anger to sweetness, from the grapes of wrath to the milk of human kindness, allows the metaphor to be uplifted, but at the cost of its structural integrity. The novel is made to close with a forced image of optimism and brotherhood, with an audacious upbeat that cries out in the wilderness. I have no wish to deny the value or the real power of good men, optimism, or brotherhood. The point is that Steinbeck imposes an unsupported conclusion upon materials which themselves are thinned out and manipulated. The increasingly grotesque episodes (and their leading metaphors) prove that even thin and manipulated materials resist the conclusion that is drawn from them, for art visits that revenge on its mistaken practitioners.

To argue that no better conclusion was available at the time, granting the country's social and political immaturity and its economic innocence, simply switches the issue from art to politics. No artist is obliged to provide solutions to the problems of the socio-politico-economic order, however "engaged" his work may be. Flaubert did not present a socioeducational program to help other young women to avoid Emma Bovary's fate. The business of the artist is to present a situation. If he manipulates the materials or forces them to conclusions that violate credibility—especially if he has a visible design upon us—his work will thin, the full range of human possibility will not be available to him, and to that extent he will have failed as an artist.

We must not exclude the likelihood, not that Steinbeck had no other conclusion at hand, but that his predisposition was to see a resolution in the various allegorical and panoramic arrangements that close out *The Grapes of Wrath*; Steinbeck's earlier work argues for that likelihood.

Yet that is not all there is to John Steinbeck. If he becomes the willing victim of abstract, horrendously schematic manipulations as *The Grapes of Wrath* nears its close still he is capable of better things. He demonstrates these potentialities particularly in minor scenes dealing with minor characters, so the negative force of the imposed conclusion is lessened.

Consider the scene in which Ruthie and Winfield make their way (along with the family) from the flooded boxcar to the barn where Rose of Sharon will feed the sick man. The intention of the scene is programmatic: the children's identification with the group concept. The overt content is the essentially undamaged survival of their sense of fun and of beauty. Significantly, the action makes no directly allegorical claim on the reader, unlike the rest of the concluding scenes.

Ruthie finds a flower along the road, "a scraggly geranium gone wild, and there was one rain-beaten blossom on it." The common flower, visualized, does not insist on the identity of the beaten but surviving beauty in pure nature with the uprooted, starved children of all the migrants. The scene is developed implicitly, in dramatic, imagistic terms. Ruthie and Winfield struggle to possess the petals for playthings, and Ma forces Ruthie to be kind:

> Winfield held his nose near to her. She wet a petal with her tongue and jabbed it cruelly on his nose. "You little son-of-a-bitch," she said softly. Winfield felt for the petal with his

fingers, and pressed it down on his nose. They walked quickly after the others. Ruthie felt how the fun was gone. "Here," she said. "Here's some more. Stick some on your forehead."

The scene recapitulates the earlier scene on the playground of the government camp. Here, as there, Winfield is the innocent, and Ruthie's cruelty is changed by external pressure (the other children, Ma's threat) to an official kindness that transcends itself to become a genuine kindness when "the fun was gone." The observed basis of the present scene is the strained relationship, that usually exists between an older sister and a younger brother. There is no visible effort to make the scene "fit" a predetermined allegorical scheme. Ruthie's kind gesture leads into Rose of Sharon's, as child to adult, and both scenes project the affirmative values—the survival of optimism, brotherhood, kindliness, goodness—that are the substance of the group concept at the conclusion. The children's quarrel and reconciliation is a relatively unloaded action, an event in itself. Tom's affirmation is nondramatic, a long, deeply mystical speech to Ma. Rose of Sharon's affirmation is out of character and frankly incredible. Uncle John's symbolic action derives from his own guilt but expresses a universal anger.

As the scene between the children is exceptional, Steinbeck's development of the flood scene is typical. Allegorical intentions override narrative power: the family's struggle against the flood is intended to equate with its surviving will to struggle against hopelessness; Pa, Uncle John, and Al are exhausted but not beaten. Tom's insight precedes the flood; Rose of Sharon's agreement to breastfeed the sick man follows it. In the larger frame, neither extreme of drouth or flood can exhaust the will and the vitality of the people. The dense texture of these panoramic materials is impressive. They lie side by side, at different levels of the "willing suspension of disbelief," depending on whether they are convincing narrative actions or palpable links in an arranged allegory. Hence, there is no great sense of a concluding "knot," an organic fusion of parts; there is no more than a formulated ending, a pseudoclose that does not convince because its design is an a priori assertion of structure, not the supportive and necessary skeleton of a realized context. Here structure and materials fail to achieve a harmonious relationship.

These final scenes are not hackwork. We cannot apply to Steinbeck, even here, the slurring remark that F. Scott Fitzgerald aimed at Thomas Wolfe: "The stuff about the GREAT VITAL HEART OF AMERICA is just simply corny." Steinbeck's carefully interwoven strands of character, metaphor, and narrative argue a conscious, skillful intention, not a sudden lapse of material or of novelistic ability. Even in failure, Steinbeck is a formidable technician. His corn, here, if it exists, is not a signal of failed ability.

Steinbeck's feeling that *The Grapes of Wrath* must close on an intense level of sweetness, of optimism and affirmation, is not seriously in doubt. His ability to use the techniques of structure to this end is evident. The earlier novels demonstrate his able willingness to skillfully apply an external structure, to mold, or at least to mystify, somewhat recalcitrant materials. The letter withdrawing *L'Affaire Lettuceburg* suggests that Steinbeck is aware of having that willing skill—"just twisting this people out of shape"—and of having to resist its lures in this most serious work. So for the critic there is a certain horrid fascination in Steinbeck's consistent, enormously talented demonstration of aesthetic failure in the last quarter of *The Grapes of Wrath*.

The failure is not a matter of "sprawling asides and extravagances," or the more extreme motivational simplicities of naturalism, or a lapse in the remarkably sustained folk idiom and the representative epic scope. The failure lies in the means Steinbeck utilizes to achieve the end.

The first three quarters of the novel are masterful. Characters are presented through action; symbolism intensifies character and action; the central theme of transformation from self to group develops persuasively in a solid, realized documentary context. The final quarter of the novel presents a difference in every respect. Characters are fitted or forced into allegorical roles, heightened beyond the limits of credibility, to the point that they thin out or become frankly unbelievable. Scenes are developed almost solely as links in an allegorical pattern. Texture is reduced to documentation, and allegorical signs replace symbolism. The result is a hollowed rhetoric, a manipulated affirmation, a soft twist of insistent sentiment. These qualities deny the conceptual theme by simplifying it, by reducing the facts of human and social complexity to simple opposites.

The reduction is not inherent in the materials, which are rendered magnificently in earlier parts of the novel. The reduction is the consequence of a structural choice—to apply allegory to character, metaphor, and theme. In short, *The Grapes of Wrath* could conceivably have a sweetly positive conclusion without an absolute, unrestrained dependence on allegory. Yet the least subtle variety of that highly visible structural technique, with its objectionably simplified, manipulative ordering of materials, is precisely the element that prevails in the final part of *The Grapes of Wrath*.

Why? Steinbeck is aware of various technical options, and he is able to make use of them earlier in the novel. As we have seen in the previous novels, with the exception of *In Dubious Battle*, Steinbeck draws on allegory to stiffen or to heighten fictions that are too loose—too panoramic—to achieve the semblance of a dramatic structure purely by means of technique. Apparently Steinbeck was not offended aesthetically by the overwhelming artificiality that results from an extreme dependence on allegory. That the contemporary naturalistic or symbolic novel requires a less simple or rigid structure clearly escapes Steinbeck's attention.

On the contrary, Steinbeck is greatly attracted to some extreme kind of external control in much of the immediately preceding work and in much of the succeeding work. During the rest of his career, Steinbeck does not attempt seriously, on the massive scale of *The Grapes of Wrath*, to achieve a harmonious relationship between structure and materials. He prefers some version of the control that flaws the last quarter of *The Grapes of Wrath*.

This judgment offers a certain reasonableness in the otherwise wild shift from *The Grapes of Wrath* to the play-novelettes.

KENNETH D. SWAN

The Enduring Values of John Steinbeck's Fiction: The University Student and The Grapes of Wrath

The world has changed dramatically since Steinbeck wrote *The Grapes of Wrath* in the thirties. Our age is an age of affluence contrasted to a time in the novel of poverty and hostile environment. Ours is an age of internationalization contrasted to the local, the regional, and the provincial. Ours is an urban age contrasted to the rural and the agrarian; an age of education contrasted to the age of the unlearned and the uneducated; an age of technology and the computer contrasted to the backwoods and the unsophisticated, an age of science fiction contrasted to the realism of the Dust Bowl and the Great Depression. So why do the students of the nineties still read the fiction of John Steinbeck? Certainly, there is always the intriguing appeal of the long ago and far away, but *The Grapes of Wrath* does not fit well in the genre of the literature of nostalgia. Its realism is too brutal for that, and its naturalistic detail too discomforting in its vivid portrayal of the dehumanization of character and the destruction of the Joad family despite their heroism. So why are university students still intrigued with John Steinbeck? I asked that question of several of my students, and I discovered that there was a consensus in their responses and that they find enduring values that have broad appeal to today's university students.

From *The Critical Response to John Steinbeck's* The Grapes of Wrath, ed. Barbara A. Heavilin. © 2000 by Greenwood Press. Reproduced with permission of Greenwood Publishing Group, Inc., Westport, CT and the author.

Accustomed to an organizational structure involving plot development or character delineation, students are initially troubled with the organization of *The Grapes of Wrath* around situations rather than plot or character. Organized as it is against a backdrop of the panoramic and scenic, the detail, symbols, dramatization, and choric effects in *GW* are techniques designed for the portrayal of situation, not plot or character. Therefore, description often substitutes for narration. The successive situations—the drought in Oklahoma, the journey west on Highway 66, and the oppression and hardship in California—are panoramic and constitute the essential structure of the novel. These situations are basically scenes which must be depicted or described, not actions that must be narrated or dramatized. Students often note that Steinbeck's tendency toward panoramic vision makes this book (and others of his) highly memorable and easily adapted to film. The scenes are layered with images which are rich with realistic details and with creative imagination which appeal to the aesthetic sense of the student. Who can forget the stark images of Mule Graves creeping in the shadows of an abandoned house; of Grampa being buried in the dirt along the roadside; of the contempt of the men who spit and swear and say about the Joads, "They aint human"; of the displaced families in Hooverville looking desperately for work, any kind of work; of the bludgeoning death of Jim Casy, that gentle prophet; of the Joad truck mired in the mud swept by the flooding river; of the loss of Rosasharn's stillborn baby and the dramatic, symbolic nurturing of a starving, dying man? These images burn themselves into the mind and form a lasting memory. To students, these images are brutal but unforgettable.

Another enduring value of *The Grapes of Wrath* is its symbolic texture, its biblical parallels. Even though some of the parallels are transformed, the texture of this novel is rich with biblical symbols which strengthen the unity of the novel and enhance its thematic structure. Steinbeck's ability to select an archetypal situation and shape it into his own story dramatizes the universality of human behavior and the cyclical recurrence of human situations and human responses. Students observe the Biblical patterns in many of Steinbeck's works, including the disturbing parallel to Judas, the betrayer, in *The Winter of Our Discontent*; the multifaceted parallel to Cain and Abel in *East of Eden*; and in *The Grapes of Wrath* the dramatic parallel to the children of Israel, an impoverished people's leaving Egypt for the promised land. The Joads leave Oklahoma, where they have been victimized by circumstances beyond their control, and sojourn to a new land, led by a charismatic leader, Jim Casy.

Peter Lisca and Joseph Fontenrose have discussed these parallels at length. Fontenrose, for instance, states that the name Joad is meant to suggest Judah (75). Readers have long identified Jim Casy with Moses or with Jesus Christ. Certainly, John Steinbeck does not want the reader to miss these parallels since he appropriately selects a biblical phrase for the book's title, and he structures his story after the exodus of the Hebrews from Egypt to Canaan. As critics have pointed out, the drought, the journey, and the sojourn in California, the three main divisions of the book, follow the pattern of the biblical exodus of the children of Israel. At my university, where students are steeped in biblical literature, they often trace these biblical parallels in insightful papers which delineate the Joads as the chosen people who suffer oppression and denial in the land where they had lived for generations and who meet with hostility and conflict in the land of their destination. The unwritten code of the migrant camps is reminiscent of Mosaic law, and Rose of Sharon's stillborn child, set adrift upon a stream, reminds the reader of baby Moses floating in a basket made of bulrushes. Biblical parallels are extensive, providing depth and variety that enrich the fabric of the text and provide multiple levels of reading for the student who enjoys searching out the parallels, as inverted as they are at times.

The thematic structure of *The Grapes of Wrath* also offers considerable fascination for students because Steinbeck dramatizes a cluster of ideas which have less to do with social and economic causes and more to do with human worth, meaning, and value. The attention that Steinbeck gives to the idea of the transcendental unity of all humanity is a welcome contrast to today's emphasis on the individual and solitary. Understanding this concept of unity, commonalities, and responsibility constitutes the primary education of the Joad family as well as the chief message of Jim Casy. This concept offers the opportunity to introduce students to Victor Frankl as well, who maintains that America needs a Statue of Responsibility on the west coast to balance the Statue of Liberty on the east coast. The contentions of these two writers, both of whom are concerned with what it means to be truly human—one a writer by profession and the other a Jewish psychiatrist who endured and survived the Nazi death camps during the

Holocaust—work in concert with one another, their ideas reverberating, the one authenticating the other. And, painful as this pairing may be in showing human beings at their worst, it provides today's students a way of focusing on their own humanity. Like the Joads, to use Warren French's depiction, they are introduced to an "education of the heart."

French re-titles *The Grapes of Wrath* as "The Education of the Heart" and discusses the theme of universal brotherhood, as taught by Jim Casy, which in the course of the plot transforms the behavior of the Joads from ignorance and selfish clannishness to enlightenment and unity with others (107). In Casy's words, "a fella ain't got a soul of his own, but on'y a piece of a big one." This concept of spiritual unity, contrasting sharply to the physical reality of everything's falling apart, places the novel squarely in the tradition of the transcendental literature of Emerson, Thoreau, and Whitman (as Frederick Carpenter points out in "The Philosophical Joads"). This primary theme is one of the unifying forces within the novel and gives the work a level of meaning that engages the theoretical and intellectual. Other critics, such as Alfred Marks, interpret this theme in a biological or microcosmic sense (74). The individual is not only a part of a specific group but a part of the macrocosm of humanity. The Joad family members mold into a mass of migrating humanity.

A third thematic consideration is Casy's moral philosophy— "There ain't no sin and there ain't no virtue. There's just the stuff people do." Casy's rejection of absolute moral principles to judge the conduct of people leads him to a relativistic, humanistic view of life. Critics have made much of Steinbeck's non-teleological thought and his reluctance to think in cause-and-effect terms (Marks 77). Although the typical college student reading Steinbeck has read little literary criticism, Steinbeck's dramatization of the key ideas of transcendental unity, group identity, "is thinking," and moral ambiguity stimulate thoughtful responses from thoughtful students, who are led to reflect on their own place in relation to others.

Steinbeck's human sympathy for characters robbed of their human dignity in a hostile environment is readily evident, and students relate well to the underdog or victim, often with a strong sense of injustice. Even though the Joads are far removed in terms of time, place, and social position, they represent heroic losers, who despite their ignorance and narrowness develop in positive ways. In the novel, a contrast is established between the negative, naturalistic force of events that threaten the Joad family's physical survival, and the positive movement of the strength and beauty of the human spirit demonstrated as they accept, believe, and act out the spiritual vision of Jim Casy. The Joads are not simply naturalistic victims of their environment, but they are heroic losers. They do suffer calamitous events which are destructive of almost everything that they value. They lose their land, Grampa and Granma die, they are out of work, always looking for a job, Noah and Connie wander off, the truck mires down in the mud, Rose of Sharon's baby is born dead, and the family is deeply fragmented. But, in faith and defiance, Ma Joad exclaims, "We are the people. We go on."

Steinbeck reveals a sense of compassion for their unfortunate plight. In like manner, students respond with identification and compassion. In comparison to student response to a Charles Dickens novel, there is not the sentimentality or deep sense of compassion as for Oliver, but there is a sense of moral outrage for the injustice done to the Joads: "They were hungry, and they were fierce. And they had hoped to find a home, and they found only hatred." Steinbeck's own ethos and sense of moral outrage often is expressed in objective terms within the interchapters which serve to reinforce his ideas and to unify the microcosm of the novel in its relation to the macrocosm. To this strong sense of outrage, students relate.

Another enduring value of *GW* for the American university student is the focus on the American scene and social criticism. The context of *The Grapes of Wrath* is America in the 30s, the Great Depression, the failure of farms in the Dust Bowl, and the consequent migration to California, the land of promise. A slice of history portraying the hardship and human cost of hard times forms the basis of this story. In addition to the American setting, Steinbeck comes to the novel with clusters of American values and attitudes. Carpenter, as has been noted, shows that the novel reflects typically American ideas and ideals—Jefferson's agrarianism, Emerson's self-reliance, Whitman's love of the masses, and William James' pragmatism (324–325). Certainly, the western migration, the dream of California as a land of promise, the individualism, the free market system, the emphasis on the rights of the worker, the raw conflict, and the turmoil, restlessness, and yearning of the American characters within the book make this novel a unique representation of our country at a specific time and place. Even the idealism of Jim Casy and the unfaltering hope of the Joads to find a better place hint at doctrine of Manifest Destiny, which spiritualizes the role which people play in shaping their future and the character of their country.

Yet Steinbeck does not let America off easy, and students are often startled by the social criticism, perhaps because it challenges their view of their nation. In *The Grapes of Wrath*, America is a chaotic place governed by greed, self-interest, and a relentless hunger for land and money. Steinbeck writes:

> Once California belonged to Mexico and its land to Mexicans; and a horde of tattered feverish Americans poured in. And such was their hunger for land that they took the land—stole Sutter's land, Guerrero's land.... And these things were possession, and possession was ownership. The Mexicans were weak and fed. They could not resist, because they wanted nothing in the world as ferociously as the Americans wanted land. (231)

Also, America is a place which exploits the labor and the labor market:

> Now farming became industry, and the owners followed Rome.... They imported slaves, although they did not call them slaves: Chinese, Japanese, Mexicans, Filipinos. They live on rice and beans, the business men said. They don't need much. They wouldn't know what to do with good wages. Why look how they live. Why, look what they eat. And if they get funny—deport them. (232)

And America is a place of conflict, violence, and hatred. Steinbeck speaks of the Okies who are "seven generations back Americans" and yet are hated because they are impoverished, concluding that

> when property accumulates in too few hands it is taken away. And that companion fact: when a majority of the people are hungry and cold they will take by force what they need. And the little screaming fact that sounds through all history: repression works only to strengthen and knit the repressed. (238)

Another value of Steinbeck's fiction to which students relate is the spiritual search for values and meaning. This observation is not surprising because the most fundamental of all human problems is to discover the meaning and value of life, to deal with the reality of evil, and to discern the nature of man and God. This spiritual search is portrayed in characters such as Jim Casy, who struggles with the hypocrisy within himself, his responsibilities toward others, and his definition of the human soul. The Joads move from selfishness to servanthood, a psychic journey typical of much of Steinbeck's fiction. The servant-philosopher, Lee, in *East of Eden*, for example, struggles with the reality of the human soul and the interpretation of the biblical word 'Timshel.' This same novel prods the conscience with the recurrent theme: Am I my brother's keeper? In *The Winter of Our Discontent*, Ethan Allen Hawley, like Judas, follows his baser animal nature and betrays his wife, his friend, and his boss, but finally in a moment of regret and desperation, wills that his daughter not be corrupted by evil as he has. In *The Grapes of Wrath*, Jim Casy serves as the seeker and philosopher who interprets for the Joads not only the meaning of their changing circumstances but their role and relationship to others. Actually, he is more of a seeker than a preacher, but he has enormous influence, especially on Tom Joad and Ma Joad. Through his death Tom Joad and others are transformed, expanding a narrow, provincial concept of family to include all humankind. His ideals and ideas, then, live on through others. It is interesting to note, however, that typically, Steinbeck's philosophers are seekers, not those with "the answer" or "the solution" to life's problems.

In addition to identification with this spiritual search, my students often are puzzled by what Steinbeck's own philosophical position is and what he really believes in terms of the meaning and value of life. Because Steinbeck subscribes to no orthodox system of beliefs, they are often frustrated in their search, for he proves to be an illusive and enigmatic author. For he himself is a seeker, and his belief system continues to shift throughout his lifetime. Is the author's philosophical position the same in *East of Eden* as in *The Grapes of Wrath*? Is Jim Casy Steinbeck's persona or spokesman in *The Grapes of Wrath*? Many critics think so. What about the servant philosopher Lee in *East of Eden*? Does his search reflect the philosophical search of the author? Are his conclusions the conclusions of the author? What is Steinbeck's own position concerning determinism and freedom? Why is Lee so jubilant in discovering that the word "timshel" may be interpreted 'thou mayest' rather than 'thou shalt'? These and other questions continue to tantalize the student of Steinbeck.

No novelist succeeds unless he is a skilled storyteller, a craftsman who creates a powerful story which lingers in the mind and forms a lasting memory. And my students find that one of the most enduring values of Steinbeck's fiction is that his stories are memorable. To read *The Grapes of Wrath* or *East of Eden* is not only to read two of Steinbeck's greatest novels but also to enter a time and place distinguished both by infinite detail and particularity as well as general truth and universality. Steinbeck says of his own writing, "My whole work drive has been aimed at making people understand each other." His typical approach is to create a contemporary story based on an ancient archetype, or a universal pattern of human behavior, and it is often this fusion of an ancient story with a modern one that makes his fiction so memorable.

In addition, Steinbeck's acute sense of the dramatic and cinematic infiltrates his texts, particularly at points of crisis or climax. Recall the ending of the story *The Flight* when Pepe, the boy-man pursued for killing a man and now trapped in the mountains, dramatically stands, unprotected, to face the consequences of his actions. Recall the final scene in *Of Mice and Men* with George and Lennie. George, fearful of what the vigilantes will do to Lennie when they catch him, takes the life of his friend, as he tenderly verbalizes their shared dreams and wishes. Recall the crisis of *East of Eden* when the scheming Cal takes his brother, the innocent Aron, to see their mother Kate, the madam of a brothel. Recall also the dramatic ending to *The Grapes of Wrath*, the extraordinary gesture of Rose of Sharon in saving a dying man. Steinbeck's use of the dramatic is heightened with symbolism and irony. His reversals of fortune border on the Sophoclean. When everything is lost—when there is nothing left to, cling to—then there is a triumph of the human spirit, a glimpse into the meaning of things. My students relate well to this dramatic vision.

Critics have noted the infinite variety in the Steinbeck's work, and he says of his own writing,

> My experience in writing has followed an almost invariable
> pattern. Since by the process of writing a book I have

outgrown that book, and since I like to write, I have not written two books alike.... If a writer likes to write, he will find satisfaction in endless experimentation with his medium, ... techniques, arrangements of scenes, rhythms of words, rhythms of thought. (*Saturday Review*)

Peter Lisca speaks of Steinbeck's work as being remarkable not only for the variety but for the range of its "achievements in prose style as different as *In Dubious Battle* and *Tortilla Flat*; in structure as different as *The Pearl* and *The Grapes of Wrath*; in materials as different as *The Pastures of Heaven* and *Cannery Row*; in sentiment as different as *The Pearl* and *The Grapes of Wrath*" (293–294). While some critics have been offput by Steinbeck's thus refusing to be pigeonholed, my students respond positively to this wide range of prose styles.

Finally, Steinbeck's simplicity, imagination, and raw power in characterizing the elemental realities of the human heart in stories such as *The Red Pony* and *The Pearl*, short novels to which students are probably first introduced in high school, have left a memorable impact. When I ask, "How did you feel in response to reading this book? the invariable answer comes, "I felt sad." A simple answer but a good response. I have to admit that on my first reading of the plight of the Joads, the loss, the hatred, the suffering, the injustice, the dehumanization, I experienced anger and a deep sense of injustice. Students, too, often express an experience of a deep sense of anger and injustice in reading *The Grapes of Wrath*. Steinbeck plays to the elemental emotions, and my students identify with his powerful depiction of the human struggle.

Juliana Menges, a 1999 graduate of Taylor University, describes her experience with Steinbeck's fiction, maintaining that she finds herself attracted to his works because

> he seems to create elaborate puzzles to which there is not any one solution—the dimensions overlap and yet depend upon each other. Each time I read one of Steinbeck's books I understand more about the man himself and his intentions for the work. Steinbeck was not meant to be neatly defined; instead, he transcends and soars above conventional definitions. He is not neat and tidy.

Nor is *The Grapes of Wrath* "neat and tidy." My students are challenged by its layers of meaning and quite willing to explore them, in part because they are in search of themselves, their own identity and meaning. Steinbeck's vivid depiction of time and place, then, is a powerful dramatization of a harsh era which rises above time and place. As a parable of the strength and beauty of the human spirit, it achieves universal value. Such a story will always appeal to readers regardless of time, place, and relentless change. My students have discovered in the Steinbeck aesthetic a consideration and enactment of those vital principles that remind us of our humanity. In his characters who have come to occupy a mythic place in the national identity, in his focus on the American scene that further tells us who we are, in his social criticism that takes us on a spiritual search and that gives us a glimpse of who we can be or should be, my students find a challenge for both mind and heart.

References

Astro, Richard. *John Steinbeck and Edward F. Ricketts*. Minneapolis: The University of Minnesota Press, 1973.

Carpenter, Frederick I. "The Philosophical Joads." *College English 2* (January 1941): 324–325.

Fontenrose, Joseph. *John Steinbeck: An Introduction and Interpretation*. New York: Barnes and Noble, 1963.

French, Warren. *John Steinbeck*. New York: Twayne Publishers, 1961.

Lisca, Peter. *The Wide World of John Steinbeck*. New Brunswick, New Jersey: Rutgers University Press, 1958.

Marks, Lester Jay. *Thematic Design in the Novels of John Steinbeck*. The Hague: Mouton, 1969.

Menges, Juliana. "One Student's Response to Steinbeck." Taylor University, June 1998.

Steinbeck, John. "Critics, Critics Burning Bright," *The Saturday Review of Literature* 33 (11 Nov. 1950): 20–21.

Steinbeck, John. "Letter to Literary Agent." In *The Wide World of John Steinbeck* by Peter Lisca. January 1937.

Chronology

Feb. 27, 1902	John Ernst Steinbeck III is born.
1918	Nearly dies from pneumonia.
1919	Graduates from high school and enters Stanford University.
1919-1925	Works at various jobs and attends Stanford sporadically.
1926	Goes to New York City and works at various jobs, including reporting.
1927	Works on Lake Tahoe and publishes his first short story.
1928	Finishes his first novel, *Cup of Gold* and works at a fish hatchery, where he meets Carol Henning.
1929	*Cup of Gold* is published.
1930	Steinbeck and Henning are married.
1932	*The Pastures of Heaven* is published.
1933	"The Red Pony" appears in the *North American Review*.
1934	Steinbeck's mother dies.
1935	Steinbeck's father dies, and he writes *Tortilla Flat*.
1936	*In Dubious Battle* is published. *Of Mice and Men* is written.
1937	*Of Mice and Men* is published and is chosen to be Book-of-the-Month Club selection.

1938	*Their Blood Is Strong,* a non-fiction account of the migrants in California, is published; Steinbeck writes *The Grapes of Wrath.*
1939	*The Grapes of Wrath* is published and becomes a bestseller.
1942	*Bombs Away: The Story of a Bomber Team* is published.
1943	Steinbeck divorces Henning, marries Gwyndolyn Conger.
1944	Writes *Cannery Row,* and son Thom is born.
1945	*Cannery Row* is published; Steinbeck works on the movie script for *The Pearl.*
1946	Second son, John Steinbeck IV, is born.
1947	*The Pearl* is published.
1948	Divorces Conger.
1950	Marries Elaine Scott; *Burning Bright* is published.
1951	Writes *Journal of a Novel* and completes the first draft of *East of Eden.*
1952	*East of Eden* is published, and Steinbeck works for Adlai Stevenson's election campaign.
1954	*Sweet Thursday* is published, and Steinbeck has his first heart attack.
1955	Steinbeck and wife Elaine move to Sag Harbor.
1957	*The Short Reign of Pippin IV: A Fabrication* is published.
1959	Steinbeck suffers a stroke.
1960	Travels around the U.S. and writes *Travels with Charley.*
1961	*The Winter of Our Discontent,* his last novel, is published; Steinbeck has another heart attack.
1962	Receives the Nobel Prize for literature.
1963	Travels with Elaine to the Soviet Union. John F. Kennedy is assassinated.
1965	His younger sister Mary dies.
1966	John Steinbeck IV goes to Vietnam; *America and Americans* is published; Steinbeck and Elaine travel to Vietnam as correspondents for *Newsday.*

1967   Has back surgery, and his son is arrested—and
            eventually acquitted—on possession of marijuana
            charges.

1968   Health deteriorates; he dies on December 20.

Works by John Steinbeck

Cup of Gold: A Life of Sir Henry Morgan, Buccaneer, with Occasional Reference to History, 1932.

The Pastures of Heaven, 1932.

To a God Unknown, 1933.

Tortilla Flat, 1935.

In Dubious Battle, 1936.

Of Mice and Men, 1937.

The Red Pony, 1937.

Their Blood Is Strong, 1938.

The Long Valley, 1938.

The Grapes of Wrath, 1939.

Sea of Cortez: A Leisurely Journal of Travel and Research with a Scientific Appendix. Coauthored with Edward F. Ricketts, 1941.

The Forgotten Village, 1941.

Bombs Away: The Story of a Bomber Team, 1942.

The Moon Is Down, 1942.

The Moon Is Down: A Play in Two Parts, 1942.

Cannery Row, 1945.

The Wayward Bus, 1947.

The Pearl, 1947.

A Russian Journal, 1948.

Burning Bright, 1950.

The Log from the "Sea of Cortez," 1951.

East of Eden, 1952.

Sweet Thursday, 1954.

The Short Reign of Pippin IV: A Fabrication, 1957.

Once There Was a War, 1958.

The Winter of Our Discontent, 1961.

Travels with Charley, 1962.

America and Americans, 1966.

Journal of a Novel: The "East of Eden" Letters, 1969.

Viva Zapata! (screenplay of 1952 film), 1974.

Steinbeck: A Life in Letters. Edited by Elaine Steinbeck and Robert Wallsten, 1975.

The Acts of King Arthur and His Noble Knights: From the Winchester Manuscript and Other Sources. Edited by Chase Horton, 1976.

Working Days: The Journal of "The Grapes of Wrath." Edited by Robert DeMott, 1988.

Works about John Steinbeck

Astro, Richard. *Edward F. Ricketts*. Boise, ID: Boise State University Press, 1976.

———. *John Steinbeck and Edward F. Ricketts: The Shaping of a Novelist*. Minneapolis, MN: University of Minnesota Press, 1973.

———, and Joel W. Hedgpeth, eds. *Steinbeck and the Sea*. Corvallis, OR: Oregon State University Press, 1975.

———, and Tetsumaro Hayashi, eds. *Steinbeck: The Man and His Work*. Corvallis: Oregon State University Press, 1971.

Beegal, Susan F., Susan Shillinglaw, and Wesley N. Tiffney, Jr., eds. *Steinbeck and the Environment: Interdisciplinary Approaches*. Tuscaloosa, AL: University of Alabama Press, 1997.

Benson, Jackson J. *Looking for Steinbeck's Ghost*. Norman, OK: University of Oklahoma Press, 1988.

———. *Steinbeck's "Cannery Row": A Reconsideration*. Muncie, IN: Steinbeck Essay Series No. 4, 1991.

———. *The True Adventures of John Steinbeck, Writer*. New York: Viking, 1984.

———, ed. *The Short Novels of John Steinbeck: Critical Essays with a Checklist to Steinbeck Criticism*. Durham, NC: Duke University Press, 1990.

Bloom, Harold, ed. *John Steinbeck*. Modern Critical Views. New York: Chelsea House, 1987.

———, ed. *John Steinbeck's "The Grapes of Wrath."* Modern Critical Interpretations. New York: Chelsea House, 1988.

Brown, Mary A. *"The Grapes of Wrath* and The Literary Canon of American Universities in the Nineties." *The Critical Response to John Steinbeck's* The Grapes of Wrath. Ed. Barbara A. Heavilin. CT: Greenwood Publishing Group, 2000.

Carpenter, Frederick I. "The Philosophical Joads." *Steinbeck and His Critics: A Record of Twenty-Five Years.* Eds. Tedlock, E.W., Jr. and C.V. Wicker. Albuquerque, NM: Vol. of New Mexico Press, 1957.

Coers, Donald V. *John Steinbeck as Propagandist: "The Moon is Down" Goes to War.* Tuscaloosa, AL: University of Alabama Press, 1991.

———, Paul D. Ruffin, and Robert J. De Mott, eds. *After "The Grapes of Wrath": Essays on John Steinbeck in Honor of Tetsumaro Hayashi.* Athens, OH: Ohio University Press, 1995.

Covici, Pascal, ed. *The Portable Steinbeck.* New York: Viking, 1971.

Crouch, Steve. *Steinbeck Country.* Palo Alto, CA: American West, 1973.

Davis, Robert Con, ed. *Twentieth Century Interpretations of "The Grapes of Wrath."* Englewood Cliffs, NJ: Prentice-Hall, 1982.

Davis, Robert Murray, ed. *Steinbeck: A Collection of Critical Essays.* Englewood Cliffs, NJ: Prentice Hall, 1972.

DeMott, Robert. *Steinbeck's Reading: A Catalogue of Books Owned and Borrowed.* New York: Garland, 1984.

———. *Steinbeck's Typewriter: Essays on His Art.* Troy, NY: Whitston Publishing, 1996.

———, ed. *Working Days: The Journals of "The Grapes of Wrath."* New York: Viking, 1989.

Ditsky, John. *Essays on "East of Eden."* Muncie, IN: Steinbeck Monograph Series No. 7, 1977.

———. *John Steinbeck and the Critics.* Camden House, 2000.

———, ed. *Critical Essays on Steinbeck's "The Grapes of Wrath."* Boston: G.K. Hall, 1989.

Enea, Sparky, as told to Audry Lynch. *With Steinbeck in the Sea of Cortez.* Los Osos, CA: Sand River Press, 1991.

Fensch, Thomas. *Steinbeck and Covici: The Story of a Friendship.* Middlebury, VT: Eriksson Press, 1979.

———, ed. *Conversations With John Steinbeck.* Jackson, MS: University Press of Mississippi, 1988.

Fontenrose, Joseph. *John Steinbeck: An Introduction and Interpretation.* New York: Holt, Rinehart and Winston, 1963.

———. *Steinbeck's Unhappy Valley.* Berkeley, CA: Joseph Fontenrose, 1981.

French, Warren. *Filmguide to "The Grapes of Wrath."* Bloomington: Indiana University Press, 1973.

———. *John Steinbeck.* New York: Twayne, 1961.

———. *John Steinbeck.* Revised edition. Boston: Twayne, 1975.

———. *John Steinbeck's Fiction Revisited.* New York: Twayne, 1994.

———. *John Steinbeck's Nonfiction Revisited.* New York: Twayne, 1996.

———, ed. *A Companion to "The Grapes of Wrath."* New York: Viking, 1963.

Galati, Frank, adaptor. *"The Grapes of Wrath."* London: Warner Chappell Plays, 1991.

Gale, Robert L. *Barron's Simplified Approach to Steinbeck: "Grapes of Wrath."* Woodbury, NY: Barron's, 1967.

Gladstein, Mimi R. *The Indestructible Woman in Faulkner, Hemingway, and Steinbeck.* Ann Arbor, MI: UMI Research Press, 1986.

Gray, James. "John Steinbeck: 1902-1968." *American Writers: A Collection of Literary Biographies.* Ed. Leonard Unger. Vol. 4. New York: Scribner's, 1974.

Hadella, Charlotte Cook. *"Of Mice and Men": A Kinship of Powerlessness.* New York: Twayne, 1995.

Hayashi, Tetsumaro. *A New Steinbeck Bibliography, 1929-1971.* Metuchen, NJ: Scarecrow Press, 1973.

———. *A New Steinbeck Bibliography, 1971-1981.* Metuchen, NJ: Scarecrow, 1983.

———. *A Student's Guide to Steinbeck's Literature: Primary and Secondary Sources.* Muncie, IN: Steinbeck Bibliography Series No. 1, 1986.

———. *John Steinbeck and the Vietnam War (Part I).* Muncie, IN: Steinbeck Monograph Series No. 12, 1986.

———. *Steinbeck's World War II Fiction, "The Moon is Down": Three Explications.* Muncie, IN: Steinbeck Essay Series No. 1, 1986.

———, ed. *A Handbook for Steinbeck Collectors, Librarians, and Scholars.* Muncie, IN: Steinbeck Monograph Series No. 11, 1981.

————, ed. *A New Study Guide to Steinbeck's Major Works, with Critical Explications*. Metuchen, NJ: Scarecrow Press, 1993.

————, ed. *A Study Guidebook to Steinbeck: A Handbook to His Major Works*. Metuchen, NJ: Scarecrow Press, 1974.

————, ed. *A Study Guidebook to Steinbeck (Part II)*. Metuchen, NJ: Scarecrow Press, 1979.

————, ed. *A Study Guide to Steinbeck's "The Long Valley."* Ann Arbor, MI: University of Michigan Press, 1976.

————, ed. *John Steinbeck on Writing*. Muncie, IN: Steinbeck Essay Series No. 2, 1988.

————, ed. *John Steinbeck: The Years of Greatness, 1936-1939*. Tuscaloosa, AL: University of Alabama Press, 1993.

————, ed. *Steinbeck's Literary Dimension: A Guide to Comparative Studies*. Metuchen, NJ: Scarecrow, 1991.

————, ed. *Steinbeck's Short Stories in "The Long Valley": Essays in Criticism*. Muncie, IN: Steinbeck Monograph Series No. 15, 1991.

————, ed. *Steinbeck's "The Grapes of Wrath": Essays in Criticism*. Muncie, IN: Steinbeck Essay Series No. 3, 1990.

————, ed. *Steinbeck's Travel Literature: Essays in Criticism*. Muncie, IN: Steinbeck Monograph Series No. 10, 1980.

————, ed. *Steinbeck's Women: Essays in Criticism*. Muncie, IN: Steinbeck Monograph Series No. 9, 1979.

————, ed. *Steinbeck and Hemingway: Dissertation Abstracts and Research Opportunities*. Metuchen, NJ: Scarecrow Press, 1980.

————, ed. *Steinbeck and the Arthurian Theme*. Muncie, IN: Steinbeck Monograph Series No. 5, 1975.

————, ed. *Steinbeck Criticism: A Review of Book-Length Studies (1939-1973)*. Muncie, IN: Steinbeck Monograph Series No. 4, 1974.

————, and Kenneth D. Swan, eds. *Steinbeck's Prophetic Vision of America*. Upland, IN: Taylor University Press, 1976.

————, and Thomas J. Moore, eds. *Steinbeck's Posthumous Work: Essays in Criticism*. Muncie, IN: Steinbeck Monograph Series No. 14, 1989.

————, and Thomas J. Moore, eds. *Steinbeck's "The Red Pony": Essays in Criticism*. Muncie, IN: Steinbeck Monograph Series No. 13, 1988.

————, Yasuo Hashiguchi, and Richard F. Peterson, eds. *John Steinbeck: East and West*. Muncie, IN: Steinbeck Monograph Series No. 8, 1978.

Hughes, R.S. *Beyond The Red Pony: A Reader's Companion to Steinbeck's Complete Short Stories*. Metuchen, NJ: Scarecrow Press, 1987.

———. *John Steinbeck: A Study of the Short Fiction*. Boston: Twayne, 1989.

Kiernan, Thomas. *The Intricate Music: A Biography of John Steinbeck*. Boston: Little, Brown Press, 1979.

Kinney, Arthur F. "The Arthurian Cycle in *Tortilla Flat*." *Steinbeck: A Collection of Critical Essays*. Ed. Robert Murray Davis. Englewood Cliffs, NJ: Prentice-Hall, 1963.

Levant, Howard. *The Novels of John Steinbeck: A Critical Study*. Columbia, MO: University of Missouri Press, 1974.

Lewis, Cliff, and Carroll Britch, eds. *Rediscovering Steinbeck: Revisionist Views of His Art, Politics and Intellect*. Lewiston, NY: Edwin Mellen Press, 1989.

Lisca, Peter. *John Steinbeck: Nature and Myth*. New York: Crowell, 1978.

———. *The Wide World of John Steinbeck*. New Brunswick, NJ: Rutgers University Press, 1958.

———, ed. *John Steinbeck: "The Grapes of Wrath": Text and Criticism*. New York: Viking, 1972.

———, and Kevin Hearle, eds. *"The Grapes of Wrath": Text and Criticism*. New York: Penguin, 1997.

McCarthy, Paul. *John Steinbeck*. New York, Ungar, 1980.

Marks, Lester Jay. *Thematic Design in the Novels of John Steinbeck*. The Hague: Mouton, 1969.

Metzger, Charles R. "John Steinbeck's Paisano Knights." *Readings on John Steinbeck*, Ed. Clarice Swisher. San Diego, CA: Greenhaven Press, 1996.

———. "Steinbeck's Mexican-Americans." *Steinbeck: The Man and His Work*. Corvallis, OR: Oregon State UP, 1971.

Meyer, Michael, ed. *The Hayashi Steinbeck Bibliography, 1982-1996*. Lanham, MD: Scarecrow Press, 1998.

Millichap, Joseph R. *Steinbeck and Film*. New York, Ungar, 1983.

Moore, Harry Thornton. *The Novels of John Steinbeck: A First Study*. Chicago: Normandie House, 1939.

Morsberger, Robert E. "Steinbeck and the Stage." *The Short Novels of John Steinbeck: Critical Essays with a Checklist to Steinbeck Criticism*, Ed. Jackson J. Benson. Durham, NC: Duke UP, 1990.

————,ed. *Zapata: A newly discovered narrative by John Steinbeck, with his screenplay of Viva Zapata!* New York: Penguin, 1993.

Noble, Donald R., ed. *The Steinbeck Question: New Essays in Criticism.* Troy, NY: Whitson Publishing, 1993.

Owens, Louis. *John Steinbeck's Re-Vision of America.* Athens, GA: University of Georgia Press, 1985.

————. *"The Grapes of Wrath": Trouble in the Promised Land.* Boston: Twayne. 1989.

Parini, Jay. *John Steinbeck: A Biography.* New York: Henry Holt, 1995.

Railsback, Brian E. *Parallel Expeditions: Charles Darwin and the Art of John Steinbeck.* Moscow, ID: University of Idaho Press, 1995.

Ross, Woodburn O. "John Steinbeck: Naturalism's Priest." *Steinbeck and His Critics: A Record of Twenty Five Years.* Eds. Tedlock, E.W. Jr., and C.V. Wicker. Albuquerque, NM: University of New Mexico Press, 1957.

Schmitz, Anne-Marie. *In Search of Steinbeck.* Los Altos, CA: Hermes Press, 1978.

Shillinglaw, Susan. "John Steinbeck." *Encyclopedia of American Literature,* Ed. Steven R. Serafin. New York: Continuum, 1999.

Simmonds, Roy. *John Steinbeck: The War Years, 1939-1945.* Lewisburg, PA: Bucknell University Press, 1996.

————. *Steinbeck's Literary Achievement.* Muncie, IN: Steinbeck Monograph Series No. 6, 1976.

Smith, Joel A., ed. *Steinbeck on Stage & Film.* Louisville, KY: Actors Theatre of Louisville, 1996.

St. Pierre, Brian. *John Steinbeck: The California Years.* San Francisco: Chronicle, 1983.

Swan, Kenneth. "The Enduring Values of John Steinbeck's Fiction: The University Student and *The Grapes of Wrath.*" *The Critical Response to John Steinbeck's* The Grapes of Wrath. Ed. Barbara Heavilin. CT: Greenwood Publishing Group, 2000.

Tedlock, E.W., Jr., and C.V. Wicker, eds. *Steinbeck and His Critics.* Albuquerque: University of New Mexico Press, 1957.

Timmerman, John H. *John Steinbeck's Fiction: The Aesthetics of the Road Taken.* Norman, OK: University of Oklahoma Press, 1986.

———. *The Dramatic Landscape of John Steinbeck's Short Stories*. Norman, OK: University of Oklahoma Press, 1990.

Weber, Tom. *Cannery Row: A Time to Remember*. Monterey, CA: Orenda/Unity, 1983.

Whitebrook, Peter. *Staging Steinbeck: Dramatizing "The Grapes of Wrath."* London: Cassell, 1988.

Wollenberg, Charles, ed. *John Steinbeck: The Harvest Gypsies*. Berkeley, CA: Heyday Books, 1988.

Wyatt, David, ed. *New Essays on "The Grapes of Wrath."* New York: Cambridge University Press, 1990.

WEBSITES

The John Steinbeck Centennial Celebration
http://www.steinbeck100.org/

Monterey County Historical Society
http://users.dedot.com/mchs/steinbeck.html

National Steinbeck Center
http://www.steinbeck.org/MainFrame.html

Nobel e-Museum: John Steinbeck Biography
http://www.nobel.se/literature/laureates/1962/steinbeck-bio.html

San Jose State University
http://www.sjsu.edu/depts/steinbec/srchome.html

Contributors

HAROLD BLOOM is Sterling Professor of the Humanities at Yale University and Henry W. and Albert A. Berg Professor of English at the New York University Graduate School. He is the author of over 20 books, including *Shelley's Mythmaking* (1959), *The Visionary Company* (1961), *Blake's Apocalypse* (1963), *Yeats* (1970), *A Map of Misreading* (1975), *Kabbalah and Criticism* (1975), *Agon: Toward a Theory of Revisionism* (1982), *The American Religion* (1992), *The Western Canon* (1994), and *Omens of Millennium: The Gnosis of Angels, Dreams, and Resurrection* (1996). *The Anxiety of Influence* (1973) sets forth Professor Bloom's provocative theory of the literary relationships between the great writers and their predecessors. His most recent books include *Shakespeare: The Invention of the Human* (1998), a 1998 National Book Award finalist, *How to Read and Why* (2000), and *Genius: A Mosaic of One Hundred Exemplary Creative Minds* (2002). In 1999, Professor Bloom received the prestigious American Academy of Arts and Letters Gold Medal for Criticism, and in 2002 he received the Catalonia International Prize.

ELLYN SANNA has authored more than 50 books, including adult non-fiction, novels, young-adult biographies, and gift books. She also works as a freelance editor and manages Scriveners' Ink, an editorial service.

MICHAEL PRICE is an Assistant Professor of English at Grove City College in Pennsylvania. In addition to his work on this volume, he has published articles in *The Explicator* and *Explorations in Renaissance Culture*.

HOWARD LEVANT is the author of *The Novels of John Steinbeck*.

KENNETH D. SWAN is a Professor Emeritus at Taylor University and has published other articles on John Steinbeck.

INDEX